Rosemary Lain-Priestley is an Ang
contributor to 'Thought for the Day' a
Radio 4. Her current work focuses on
female clergy both locally and nationally. She is also a trustee
of the Sandford St Martin Trust which promotes excellence in
religious broadcasting, and is chair of governors of a secondary
school in Tulse Hill. She was previously Associate Vicar of St Martin-
in-the-Fields and, prior to that, curate of St Paul's, Scotforth,
Lancaster. Before ordination she worked and travelled in South
Africa and, before that, was an immigration adviser. She is
married with three young children and lives in London. In rare
moments of freedom she enjoys reading modern novels, going to
the theatre and watching any television drama series that involves
counterterrorism or forensic psychology.

UNWRAPPING THE SACRED

Seeing God in the everyday

Rosemary Lain-Priestley

First published in Great Britain in 2009

Society for Promoting Christian Knowledge
36 Causton Street
London SW1P 4ST

British Library Cataloguing-in-Publication Data
A catalogue record for this book is available from the British Library

ISBN 978–0–281–06061–0

1 3 5 7 9 10 8 6 4 2

Typeset by Graphicraft Ltd, Hong Kong
Printed in Great Britain by Ashford Colour Press

Produced on paper from sustainable forests

*For my brother Andrew, always the same when
everything's different*

For our mum, who so beautifully nurtured our childhood

For Joseph Isaac Lain, already adding laughter

Contents

Contents

Acknowledgements

I could not have written a second book without the inspiration and encouragement I have received once again from those people who enabled me to write the first. They were named in *The Courage to Connect* and they know who they are. In addition this time I want to thank:

Carolyn Keen, formerly Lord Mayor of Westminster, who introduced me to so many places and people during my time as her chaplain.

Catherine Wright, for helping me to understand hinterlands. Anne Dyer, for encouraging me to see what women might bring to public space.

The governors, staff and pupils of St Martin-in-the-Fields High School for Girls for the number and variety of things they are teaching me. And the head teacher, Lesley Morrison, for allowing me to tell part of the story of her extraordinary daughter, Ebony.

The community at the school gate of St Mary's, Bryanston Square, who keep me sane in my worst Monday morning moments (and on Tuesdays, Wednesdays, Thursdays and Fridays), and understand the sacredness of sharing coffee with friends.

Those who provide the loving and generous childcare that makes my life logistically possible.

All those friends whose personal and life-giving stories have found their way into *Unwrapping the Sacred*.

Alison Barr at SPCK, for believing that I could write a second book so soon after the first; Neil Whyte for the precision and elegance of his copy-editing; Monica Capoferri for her creativity and patience with the cover design.

Sir Andrew Motion, for his generosity in allowing me to reproduce the poem 'Now traveller, whose journey passes through'.

And, as ever, Antony, Hannah, Olivia and Joseph, for their graciousness, acceptance and love.

Introduction

———◆◆◆———

'The same same but different!' is the favourite cry of Indonesian stall-holders. They mean that what's on sale here is better than you'll get next door, perhaps higher quality or a more attractive deal.

It's also a phrase that could describe how it feels to live a human life. In different measure, depending on what happens to us and how we respond, we experience 'the same same but different' as the years progress. There are threads that weave their way through: a few friendships, certain places that we revisit or never move away from, some of our commitments and passions.

And then there's the new, the strange, the emerging, the different – which might or might not feel like better quality or a more attractive deal, but is what we're given to work with. It's the stuff that forms what we are and what we will become.

We all need the headspace to process what we're learning, what we should pay attention to, what we're seeing again and again and what we're noticing for the first time. We need some sort of mechanism in our lives to allow the stuff of our dreams to emerge so that it might entwine and enliven our conscious thoughts.

Sifting the stuff of our life might mean daydreaming, writing, painting or talking to a friend. It will involve noticing things we didn't notice before and capturing thoughts that are worth just sitting with for a few moments until something emerges. If we don't do it, a lot remains unaccessed, unappreciated, maybe even deliberately avoided.

Most of us don't have the luxury of huge chunks of quiet time in a solitary place to achieve this sifting and reflecting. We may need to build some of that into our lives. Or perhaps we should let go of the assumption that it has to be done that way and simply get on with doing it differently. Whatever our approach, we need to pay honest attention to what's around and within us, whether it's exciting, mundane or deeply painful, what we've encountered before or something different. This is a way of praying, and we need to trust ourselves and our instincts about what God might be saying to us in all of it.

Unwrapping the Sacred is an attempt to reflect on the events of a year; events in the life of the world, the lives of those around me and my own life. When I started to write I had no idea what many of those events would be, which more of the same and which different. Neither did I know whether I would be the least bit inspired by any of them. I had recently finished writing *The Courage to Connect*, a book about living life deliberately and honestly and making conscious connections between things. This next book would be my way of doing that very purposefully for a year and seeing what came of it.

Meaning and understanding can emerge immediately or much more slowly. So some of what you'll find here was written pretty much in 'real time', either in preparation for a speaking engagement, as a script for BBC Radio 4's 'Thought for the Day' or for the book itself. But most of it was drawn together later using scribbled notes and newspaper cuttings, all of which became grist to the mill of reflection.

Unwrapping the Sacred takes us from one spring to the next. It charts a year in my life during which time seemed to speed up. A year when some events were a reminder of the fragility of the people around me, but also of the strength and tenacity of human nature. I gave birth to a third baby, began a salutary 'mid-life conversation' with myself, tackled some work-related vertical learning curves, and for several months feared that I was losing the plot as I struggled to keep far too many plates spinning.

The world experienced the credit crunch and the arrival in the White House of Barack Obama. The 'new atheists' waged a campaign against religious faith. Facebook and Twitter outstripped MySpace as networking tools, and the fourth series of *The Apprentice* unfolded on BBC television. Beijing hosted the Olympics amid multiple controversies, our security services continued to wrestle with the terrorist threat and the celebrity Jade Goody died a very public death. There was plenty of material to hand.

So I set out to download my life with courage and a little trepidation, and to ask what sorts of insights might emerge from the year, knowing that what happens to us and our response to it all will inevitably shape what we become, that the lives of those around us are inextricably linked to our own, that over time we will discover that we have changed considerably yet remained much as we have always been, that some of what's on offer is pretty much what we've seen before and that some is strangely, profoundly and gloriously different.

1

From March into April: equinox moments
Nothing changes, nothing stays the same

——◆◆◆——

At 05:48 on 20 March 2008 the centre of the sun was directly over the equator. On the day of the spring equinox light and darkness are pretty much of equal length everywhere on Earth. For a brief interval we are exquisitely balanced, poised and expectant, before the tipping point comes and we begin to slide gently but inexorably into the future. The shift is inevitable but what is beyond it is entirely unpredictable. We never know quite what's coming next.

Except of course that six months later there will be another equinox, this time heralding the beginning of autumn. Another day of equal light and darkness, another moment of balance and another catching of breath.

Of course for most of us there will have been countless planetary equinoxes in our lives of which we have been wholly unaware. Life is so full, so pressured, so unrelentingly busy that any sense of the planets being momentarily poised is completely lost on us! But if we do notice those points of balance they may remind us of the comforting predictability and rhythm of all that stays the same, and too the disturbing truth that time moves on and on, and with it our lives, so that the ripe opportunities of today may no longer be available to us when the next equinox comes around.

If on 20 March 2008 we had been hoping for the warm embrace of spring we were to be disappointed. The day was blustery, cold, and by the afternoon very wet. It was Maundy

Thursday, and over the weekend it would snow. Even in central London there was enough of the white stuff to stir children to a heightened state of excitement and for vicars to joke about how they had been dreaming of a white Easter.

Traditionally on Maundy Thursday the clergy of the Church of England renew their ordination vows. It's a chance to reflect on the year that's past, a time to stand still and look back, to recollect ourselves before moving on. An equinox moment. So before the blanket of snow had quite begun to descend, the day saw me heading for St Paul's Cathedral to join hundreds of my colleagues in billowing robes, lining up to take part in a service. The wind was surprisingly strong and in order to balance we all leaned into it at improbable angles. Not until we entered the cavernous sheltered space of the cathedral were we able to stand upright again.

The renewal of those vows involves looking back and acknowledging the times we have fulfilled them less than well, expressing our regret and resolving to try again. The bishop asks, 'Will you continue in the way of Christ, the head and shepherd of the Church of God, whose grace is sufficient to meet your need?', and I find myself wondering, 'Will I, and is it?' Then taking my faith in my hands with a sense of leaning into the wind once again, I reply with the others, 'By the help of God, I will.'[1]

A line is drawn under the past, not in such a way that we can forget its imperfections and insistent lessons, but such that we are released to cross from the present into the future and to try again, afresh, anew.

Individuals, organizations and communities all have their equinox moments. We might find ourselves enjoying a relationship that has reached a point of equilibrium, where we feel connected and close in the present moment, the future looking enticing and sustaining. Or we might find ourselves in a job that plays to our strengths and brings all our experience into focus. A charity might reach an equinox moment because it has fulfilled its original remit, or an institution may realize that it is so well-established and well-practised that striving for excellence is now its day-to-day business.

God creates us all with unimaginable potential. At key points in our year, in our relationships, in our development and in our lives, we pause to assess the past and dream what might be to come. We look back at where we've come from, what we've learnt, what has gone well and what has not (or has been disastrous). We wonder what life will offer us next, what opportunities we can create to stretch ourselves, whether or not we need to change something or let go of anything before we move on. We may conclude that it's time to consolidate, to rejoice and celebrate, take a different direction altogether or continue grappling with what's familiar because it still hasn't yielded all it can.

These equinox moments rarely last long. It's not that things necessarily fall apart but generally they do change. We have an idea, someone makes a decision, people become restless, the environment alters. A tipping point is reached and things move on again. Those brief moments of poise, if captured before they pass, can be opportunities to take stock. We can use them to assess whether there are things we want to leave behind as we step into the future or new ideas we want to carry forward and explore.

At some points in our life we may become acutely aware that the time we have left in a place or a situation or with a particular person is limited. Those moments can hold very particular potential.

The media was saturated in spring 2008 by reports of the primaries leading up to the United States presidential election. *The Guardian*, covering George Bush's final State of the Union address earlier in the year, noted that he found himself having to 'share the evening' with senators Hillary Clinton and Barack Obama and that he was determined 'to resist being cast as a lame-duck President'.[2] As news from across the Atlantic continued to focus on the emerging presidential candidates and their possible running mates, we could have been forgiven for thinking that Bush was no longer a key player in the life of the United States or on the world scene. Yet this had to be far from the truth. Whether or not we agree with the 'lame-duck' analysis, whether or not we approve of what President Bush achieved in his final months in office, he still had a considerable slice of the year to go, with all the potential that carried.

We don't have to be in a key political role or to live our lives on a national stage to know what it is to struggle with our own potential. We have a God-instilled desire to inhabit and fulfil it.

Sometimes we feel that we're chasing that fulfilment in very challenging circumstances. We may sense a part of us dying as a relationship founders, feel constrained by the rising stars in our workplace or be facing middle age wondering how much time is left and whether we've used wisely what we've had so far.

We can be at our most focused and effective when something in our lives is closing down and we don't know exactly what or whether anything else will open up. It's our equivalent of Bush's final year and it can make us take a long hard look at who we are, how we might achieve something that nobody else would have the knowledge and experience to achieve in the remaining time, and how we can persuade ourselves to be open to whatever might come next.

For Christians, Holy Week and Easter recall key equinoxes and tipping points in the life of the world. When on Maundy Thursday in the garden of Gethsemane Jesus wrestles with the question of what he must do with his potential, the answer will reverberate through history. At this point on the trajectory of his life, could he choose to turn back? The Gospels seem to suggest so, as they describe the agony of his indecision while the disciples wait and repeatedly fall asleep.

He can either go to the cross or at this eleventh hour flee and therefore cease to be who he is or to live out what he is for. He can embrace the consequences of other people's hate, fear and incomprehension, or avoid that reality and create an ending to the story easier on the ear but completely disconnected from the rest of his life.

What difference does it make to us that Jesus made the choice he did? In the simplicity of childhood I sang with utter acceptance the lines of the hymn,

> He died that we might be forgiven,
> He died to make us good;
> That we might go at last to heaven,
> Saved by his precious blood.
>
> There was no other good enough
> To pay the price of sin;
> He only could unlock the gate
> Of heaven, and let us in.[3]

I believed it all, without question and without interpretation beyond accepting that it was part of some divine–cosmic equation
that had to be balanced.

But over the years my picture of God has changed so radically that I can no longer sing these words without fundamentally reinterpreting them. I don't believe that Christ's death was
part of a heavenly bargain between God the Father and God the
Son in which the punishment for sin had to be exacted and
God offered himself to himself as the sacrificial lamb. It isn't that
I can't believe God would make such a sacrifice, it's that the
idea of God insisting on an act of punitive restitution cuts right
across my understanding of the generosity and grace of our
Creator.

I also struggle with simple interpretations of the profound
truths that the writers of the Gospels and St Paul are trying to
unfold, particularly about our 'salvation history'; that is, the
way in which we can be in relationship with God in spite of our
obvious differences. It seems to me that the truths explored in
scripture are profound and complex: we glimpse shafts of light
and intricate pieces of puzzle that are part of a larger picture. It
is all very nuanced and tantalizing.

So when we read the scriptures as chronological history and
conclude that all was created perfect, went crashingly wrong
and was put right by Jesus (in spite of how it appears), it seems to
me that we are misreading as simple and linear a history more
like a figure of eight. If the wrongs of past and future were somehow healed on Good Friday, then what Jesus did reverberates
backwards through time as well as forwards. In a sense we were
always beyond Christ's decision. This is not straightforward
history of the time-constrained variety.

Good Friday and Easter are cosmic tipping points because
the whole sweep of the Christian story shows them to be such
moments. But what they signify is that it was always true that
we are whole and healed, creative and free, wounded and wounding. Equally, it is as true here and now that we are wounded
and wounding and far less than our best; that the world needs
healing and that God has healed us.

Good Friday is real. Such anguish, terror, pain and abandon-
ment will always be part of our experience in this life. But Easter

is just as true and we live that truth in our experiences of joy, creativity, wonder, peace and the sheer miracle of life.

All of these things touch on our greatest hopes and fears about our mortality and what will survive beyond it. The poet Andrew Motion says that he would like to believe in God but doesn't because he can't believe in the afterlife.[4] The two beliefs are inextricable for him, and I imagine for most of us. The question to which we all want an answer is: what was beyond the tipping point of Christ's death and what does that mean for us?

I was 32 weeks pregnant that Easter weekend in 2008, and having had two precarious past experiences of childbirth had negotiated an elective caesarean this time. But what should have been a routine antenatal check-up in Holy Week provoked a turmoil of doubt when a consultant I hadn't seen before questioned my decision.

Suggesting that I might be risking major surgery unnecessarily he told me bluntly, 'Of course you'd have a longer hospital stay and you have to be mindful about MRSA these days – you really don't want to end up with that.' Having decided irrevocably that a natural delivery was too risky I was now stuck between a rock and a hard place! The approaching tipping point was inevitable and fears about my own mortality were, for a few days, rather too sharply focused for my comfort. And all this when I was due to take part in a radio broadcast on the subject of life after death.

A few days earlier I had been making Easter baskets with four young children when the telephone rang. 'Rosemary, it's Mark from the BBC – can we talk about the resurrection?' How do you say 'Sorry, no, I'm making baskets for chocolate mini-eggs and fluffy yellow chicks'? So I said 'yes', and we had a lengthy conversation about resurrection theology. Questions such as: 'Was the tomb *really* empty and does your faith stand or fall by it?' were interspersed with 'Mum, can I have the glue?' and the indignant cry 'She's got more eggs than me – it's not fair.'

In the relative peace and sanity of a BBC studio a couple of days later, I tried to articulate the same thoughts with rather more cogency. So does my faith stand or fall on the literal truth or otherwise of the empty tomb? And do I believe that the resurrection is a physical reality, or do I think it's 'just' spiritual? What does the ultimate tipping point catapult us towards?

I do believe that if there is life beyond death it will be a life in which we connect in some way with each other, with God and with ourselves. So much of what Jesus did and said is about relationship and encounter that it would be rather odd if the resurrection life to which he leads us were one of isolation and detachment. But I hope that we will relate much more fully and in a way that isn't constrained by physical or any other limitations; that we will be much more than we are now, not the same or less.

So my understanding of heaven is certainly that it is a real and tangible experience. But I can't pin it down and describe it in concrete terms.

Our daughter, Olivia, is four years old, loves the familiar patterns and places of her young life, and wants to believe that everything will last for ever. She interrogates us about any toy that requires batteries, needing to be reassured that they can be replaced when they run out so that the toy will still work. On holiday she is always the first to ask, 'When are we going back to London?' And she insists that she is never going to leave home even if she gets married. She wants to know that things will always stay the same.

There is a very fine balance to be achieved in making Olivia's world feel safe and constant while encouraging her to be open to new things and not to avoid the issue of endings. And never is the balance more tricky than when she asks questions about the nature of heaven: Where will it be? How will we get there? Can we take things with us?

On Easter Day the great and ancient Exsultet, or Easter proclamation, is sung at sunrise services all over the world. It tells us that this is a day 'truly blessed, when hatred is cast out, peace and justice find a home, and heaven is joined to earth and all creation reconciled'[5] to God. I don't know how the world as we know it will connect with what the scriptures speak of as a renewed creation. Will it be transformed, will it be swept up into another reality, will it come to an end and something entirely new happen? I simply don't know, because when, in Revelation, St John gives us a picture of 'a new heaven and a new earth',[6] it is not an architectural blueprint, rather a stunning and rapturous vision of something beyond our comprehension. I tell Olivia that I hope heaven will offer us some of what is familiar but also, in a very good way, what is different.

In the television documentary *Back to Beirut*, Brian Keenan revisited Lebanon, taking with him his wife and young sons. Two decades previously he had spent four and a half years being tortured and beaten as a hostage in what he subsequently wrote about as his 'evil cradling'. But he didn't go back to the place where that had happened in order to reinforce his sense that evil is perpetrated in the world. He acknowledged its reality, and the reality of the pain suffered for so many years by the people of Lebanon, but he returned in order to rediscover the beauty and life of that land.

In the ruins of the detention centre a group of young girls find him and engage him in conversation. They ask him to come back later to teach them English. He describes all this with his customary poetry: 'a cloud of butterflies descended on me, and ever so gently, ever so sweetly, tried to kidnap me all over again'. Keenan's ability to rejoice in gentleness in a place where he and others have seen so much violence is incredibly poignant. He is determined to explain to his sons that people do bad things, but that that doesn't make a place or its people all bad. Then off he goes to the source of the River Adonis to paddle in the bubbling waters and laugh with joy.

These habits of Keenan's mind speak to me of Good Friday and Easter, of the reality of degradation and beauty side by side, of the starkness of fear and of the certainty of life going on elsewhere. They remind me of what is true always: that everywhere beauty and evil co-exist, and that God and humanity together are working to release more of the beauty and eradicate more of the evil, which on one level has already been dealt with but on another is still very much a part of our experience.

Keenan's documentary also reminded me how much depends on the way we choose to interpret the world around us and communicate our experience of it to others. The stories we tell, the situations we shape and the way we use our equinox moments all have an impact on the world around us and how it will look and feel in the future.

The late New Zealand artist Colin McCahon entitled one of his major works, *Tomorrow will be the same but not as this is*. We should not underestimate how much of it will be how it will be because of the decisions we make here and now; because of our willingness to sit and reflect, to wrestle and engage in the equinox moments that come to us; because of our courage to move on from those moments by recognizing or even precipitating the tipping points; because of our ability to capture and use that momentum in such a way that we, those we love, our communities and the world are tipped gently but firmly into a better and more creative place.

2

May: the back ends of buildings
The task of mending the world

On Monday 12 May 2008, Joseph Isaac Lain was born. The elective caesarean proved to be entirely straightforward, the threat of MRSA did not materialize and we were allowed home two days later.

It's sometimes said that the birth of a child forces us up hard against questions about the friendliness, or otherwise, of life. I was pregnant with our first child on 9/11. I remember being shocked by the number of people who said to me with a sympathetic sigh what a terrible time it was to be bringing a child into the world.

There is a logic to the argument. Dreadful things happen to individuals, communities and nations. No one is immune to tragedy. Even those of us whose lives are relatively physically secure can feel vulnerable to unexpected disaster. We may not be subject to famine or tragically avoidable water-borne disease, but international terrorism has unseated our sense of security. Each time we hear that an imminent terrorist plot has been thwarted by the intelligence services, we wonder whether or, more likely, when, the day will come when such a plot isn't discovered in time.

Yet it seems a little extreme to decide that the world is so far gone we should stop populating it. Of course there are times in people's lives when their personal circumstances make it impossible for them to see beyond grief and tragedy, but for most of us, a lot of the time, life is much more of a mixture, a melting-pot of good and bad. Alongside the terror, tragedy and pain of which we are only too aware, the world offers astonishing beauty; and the glory of human beings is that we have the most tremendous capacity for creativity and joy.

Joseph was born in St Mary's Hospital, Paddington. The maternity wing looks out on a street buzzing with cafés, newsagents and offices. People hang out over coffee with friends, hurry towards the station, grab a sandwich from the deli in their lunch hour: life is busy, journeys are being made, projects discussed and goals achieved.

But from other parts of the hospital the huge plate glass windows give on to a very different view. This is the flip side of the city centre – mostly what you see are the back ends of buildings. Ubiquitous drainpipes and green-mouldy gutters, the brickwork blackened with carbon, not cleaned for years. The flat-roof extensions, many sprouting scrubby plants and weeds, others with smatterings of human detritus – a ravaged pram, packaging from various white goods, broken umbrellas – all left to rot.

For some reason this back-end view unnerves me, perhaps because it represents the world as I would rather not see it, broken, tawdry and desolate. I want the city views with new, exciting, architect-designed buildings, or warmly weathered Gothic stone. Beyond the city I want shingle beaches and autumn country lanes, sharp-scented pine forests and fields of gold. I want the dreaming spires and the green and pleasant land, not the ravaged backyard.

But the injustices, the pain, the filth, the mess and the brokenness get in the way. They stir my conscience and my compassion, and I don't know what I'm supposed to do about it.

In May 2008 I finished a year's stint as Chaplain to the Lord Mayor of Westminster. It was a year that gave me a different perspective on the place where I live (and briefly on myself, when at my first event someone who'd clearly forgotten his contact lenses exclaimed, 'We don't mind a bit of totty for our chaplain this year'!).

On one particular occasion the different faith groups in the area met to explore the nature of caring and the needs of carers in Westminster, and we were reminded of the story of Miriam. Miriam was the sister of Moses, the one who hid him in the bulrushes to avoid the consequences of Pharaoh's command to kill all newborn Hebrew boys. Jewish Midrash writings tell us that because of the merits of Miriam, a source of living water followed the Israelites throughout their 40 years in the desert.[1]

Twelve months attending events with the Lord Mayor brought me into contact with myriad Miriams, and I was struck by their many different guises. They are diplomats, business people, volunteers, carers, voluntary-sector professionals, people of faith, people of no particular faith, women, men, children. The capacity to 'build wells' of all different kinds across the diverse and complex City of Westminster amazed me.

One woman made a particular impression. I met Sarah at a gathering of carers. For decades she has cared for her twin brother who has a learning disability. She told me that having survived cancer herself a few years ago she felt so fortunate to be here, 'living on borrowed time'. And I marvelled that so much of that time is being given, without any sense of resentment but rather with grace and love, to someone else.

The prophet Micah talks of the imperative for people 'to do justice, and to love kindness, and to walk humbly with your God',[2] and that same desire and determination lies at the heart of religious faith for Christians, Jews, Muslims, Sikhs and many people of other religions. Rabbi Mark Winer of the West London Synagogue has explored the Jewish concept of *tikkun olam*, which translates as 'repairing the world'. He speaks of creation as a 'shattered urn'.[3] He believes that as 'children of the same God, created equal in God's image, we can repair the world, drawing strength from our traditional resources of love and compassion'.[4]

The world, imbued as it is with God's presence, God's intention, God's longing, needs repair. But almost before we begin we can feel pretty overwhelmed by the multiplicity and complexity of that need. As we get older the sense of drop-in-the-ocean-helplessness can really undermine our ability to focus on what we have it in our power to change. It all seemed so much simpler when, as children, we began to be aware of the brokenness of the world one issue at a time.

When I was very young my compassion was aroused mostly by the plight of small, furry creatures. I was an avid money-raiser for sick animals until around the age of nine, when I graduated to people and the developing world became my passion. New wells for Indian villagers: I could be provoked almost to apoplexy by those dear elderly ladies who insisted on telling me that 'charity begins at home', or the cynic's 'Those villagers will never know how to maintain the wells; they won't last more than a month.'

When I started work that sense of injustice was channelled into issues around immigration. The legal firm I worked for acted on behalf of refugees and clients from India and Pakistan who had been refused entry to the UK. I spent weeks in preparation for appeal cases at which my boss would try to persuade adjudicators to overturn the decisions of British officials in India, Bangladesh and Pakistan who had refused to issue visas for our clients to join their partners in the UK.

But nowadays, with an adult sense of weariness, I regret that I seem to have slumped into the mode of an armchair or at best pulpit protagonist. As a priest working in a parish where homelessness was a significant concern, I arranged the annual memorial for those who died on the streets. I tried to be informed about political and social issues and to address them in sermons when appropriate. I marched on Downing Street with 600 women clergy, led by the actor Dawn French in character as television's *Vicar of Dibley*, to raise awareness of the Make Poverty History campaign.

But none of this, nor my largely silent membership of Amnesty International, leads to potentially world-changing actions. Perhaps my role is simply to be a consciousness-raiser when I get the page-space or pulpit-time. Perhaps that is a cop-out. Perhaps all this will change over time. I'm not really sure.

What I do know is that many of us struggle with the same questions about what we can do, with our limited time and financial resources, to change what needs changing in the world. I also know that as individuals, taking into account our passions, particular insights and abilities to stick with whatever projects, we must decide to what we can respond and from what we must turn aside. *Tikkun olam* can be an uncomfortable and challenging process. The chair of the Friends of a London homelessness agency has said:

> It's common to wonder why someone might choose to sleep rough. Each of us can only guess at that for ourselves. Thank God most of us do not have to. If it were me, it might be something to do with seeing and not seeing: seeing and being able to bear no longer the hypocrisies of organized social life; preferring to make plain and open how we *all* pass by

and do not see each other; that mixture of brutal honesty and brutal dishonesty to which alcohol opens the door.[5]

Tikkun olam is about choosing to see rather than not see, and daring to see with that painful and honest clarity that will motivate us to do something to change things – or, equally painfully and honestly, to come to the conclusion that a particular situation is not for us, not now.

It's hard to see what needs doing and then decide that we simply can't do it. The arrival on our streets of the so-called 'charity muggers' hasn't made it any easier. Running the gauntlet of a busy shopping area can mean using the mantra 'No, no, sorry; I'm in a hurry; I don't have time; Not today; I can't manage another direct debit' several times over. It can leave us feeling paradoxically moved by and hardened against the amount of need 'out there'. And even if we occasionally say 'yes' it doesn't take away that sense of only ever managing to contribute a drop in the ocean of what would really make a difference. We are reminded that the world's issues are so many, so varied and so insistent that much of the time the only response we can afford is to look and see rather than just strategically avert our eyes or glaze over.

In all of our efforts at *tikkun olam* we are likely to have a sense that we are only touching the tip of the iceberg. Jesus did not meet the needs of everyone he encountered, and certainly not the needs of all the needy of first-century Palestine or even of Nazareth or Jerusalem. There were even times and places when 'he could do no deed of power',[6] possibly because of the lack of faith he encountered.

That can be a very discouraging realization. If Jesus cannot achieve all this, and he is in some sense God, what hope is there for me to make any dent in the world's suffering? Alternatively, Jesus' inability to achieve everything could put our own in perspective. If even he had to make constant, careful, sometimes spontaneous, sometimes seemingly random decisions about where to focus his energy, then it is natural that we too have to make these decisions, and struggle with them, as we go about the business of 'repairing the world'.

We are inevitably left with a sense of 'What about all the others?' What about the equivalent of those who were too far back in the crowd to have a decent chance of reaching Jesus, those who had no friends or family to carry them? Today these might be the people who find themselves losing out in what some term the National Health Service 'postcode lottery', or who lack the skills properly to access the benefits system.

I wonder what it does to us, this looking and seeing and only sometimes being able to respond. Are there only two possible outcomes, either that we will become hardened about the issues and the people they affect, or waste a lot of time and emotion feeling bad about what we can't fix? There isn't a satisfactory answer, and we will often be left without any sense of closure. But perhaps even if we can do nothing, it is better to see, because not seeing in a sense denies the existence of those who are suffering and requires us to suppress our humanity.

Perhaps what matters is how we say 'no' rather than how often. Perhaps we should make eye contact with the man with the HOMELESS AND HUNGRY sign even if we're not going to give him what he's asking for. We might convey some human warmth and sympathy rather than dehumanizing the other person by avoiding even a nod or a smile. If we're saying 'no' to the charity mugger, or the appeal in the newspaper or on the television, perhaps we should determine not to forget that there are those people with that need, so that our 'no' is not unthinking or unkind, but simply the result of realism about our resources.

There will probably be times in our lives when we do feel a strong sense, or at least a growing suspicion, that we have recognized a moment in which we might respond. In the wilderness John the Baptist cried, 'The time is at hand – believe and change the way that you live.'[7] The word he used for time was *kairos*. The *kairos* moment is the 'right' moment, a moment pregnant with the opportunity to act. Jesus used the same word to tell people that the Kingdom of God was at hand, that God's grace was on offer there and then. There will be times when we recognize a *kairos* moment, the need to act right now. It's a tipping point, a moment of equilibrium in which we can choose to weight the scales in a particular direction and create a different possible future.

But at other times we need to remember that in a sense God's opportune moment is always here and now, for God's grace is eternally on offer and the world needs mending in this moment and always. On a daily basis we need to work out to which bits of its rebuilding we can contribute, how and when. If we wait until the redesign is fully worked up, so that we can make our contribution to the most attractive aspect of the project, we will in the meantime have averted our eyes from a lot of need.

So whatever is our equivalent of the back ends of buildings, the stuff that seems so overwhelmingly impossible to tackle because, frankly, it's just so huge, numerous, complex and ugly, it is required of us not to close our eyes to it. Our challenge is to work out which particular rooftop dumping ground we might slowly start to convert into a garden by simply uprooting a few weak weeds, which backyard's rubbish we might painstakingly sift through until there is a small area in which people can rest and be renewed, which drainpipes and gutters we might begin to repair and unblock so that water can flow again.

In specifics, which individual, friend or colleague might need our attention, which member of our family needs us most right now, which community project might be able to use our skills, which organization is looking out for trustees. What is *the* issue to which we might bring our professional or entrepreneurial skills? Where might our volunteering have an impact? Which charity mugger might we actually say 'yes' to with a small standing order? Which overseas development agency might seem to be doing the sort of work we might best support?

The unclean, untidy and unkempt roofs, back walls and yards of the city represent to me the stuff in life – mine and the world's – that is both precariously hidden and sometimes shockingly revealed. In my life it's the unresolved relationships, the situations I know I can change but have failed to find the time to address, and my refusal to connect with certain people who long to be connected with because, frankly, they will absorb too much of my energy. In the world's, the back end of the city represents the untended landfill of degradation, grief, poverty and pain that is an inevitable part of human experience, and to which we have no choice but to respond, even if that simply means refusing to look away.

The harsh reality is that we will never enter most of these backyards. We will make excuses or fail to find the courage or, less blameworthily, genuinely not have the time, expertise or resources. Most of this stuff, whether half hidden or right in our faces, is stuff we will never get around to. We will not sort it, mend it, face it, address it, order it, paint it, clean it, manage it or assess its progress in any way.

This is the price of having choices about what stuff needs attention. We can allow it to overwhelm us, wilfully ignore it or make a decision to tackle the parts that most connect with us and that we are given the opportunities to change – while steeling ourselves to look the rest in the eye and not pretend it doesn't exist.

And at the times when we cannot give any energy to much of this, we need to ask whether the day-to-day commitments we *do* take on can be lived out in that same spirit, defined and shaped by the knowledge that many things count towards mending the world – small gestures of kindness towards overworked colleagues, remembering the anniversary of someone's loss or talking with someone in the bus queue who might look as though they'd appreciate it.

Tikkun olam as an attitude to life is something we can all cultivate. It doesn't have to be an additional project weighting our 'To do' list further towards impossibility. Always and anyway it can be an attitude to life. And so giving Rabbi Winer the last words: 'Every single second, every minute, every hour, every day of our lives presents the opportunity to repair the world piece by piece, peace by peace.'[8]

3

June: for the sake of friendship
Intimacy, space and exposure

———◦•◦———

Ten years ago I listened to a sermon about friendship by a preacher I had never met before. He was one of those people who could lead worship with an easy combination of formal intimacy and spacious warmth. He spoke with sensitivity and insight about emotional connection and the nature and value of friendship. Of course a heterosexual person could have preached a good sermon on the same subject, but somehow I came to the conclusion that this preacher was gay. It was as though there was something in his experience of the world that shaped and coloured his thoughts in a particular way.

In *The Philosophy of Friendship*, Mark Vernon explores the idea that gay men, through the precarious and often pain-ridden process of publicly acknowledging their sexuality, have come to value true friendship very highly. Real friends accept what we are and therefore stand with us in our essential isolation.[1]

On Midsummer Day 2008 we had the privilege of being present at the civil partnership ceremony of that priest and his partner. The ingredients of the occasion were a tastefully appointed register office in spacious green surroundings, thoughtful poetry and profound prose, a party in a beautiful garden wonderfully woven with the mellow sounds of steel pans and jazz, and many, many friends. In fact the theme of friendship underpinned the whole day.

The couple's vows, written by them for the occasion, included the words:

> I am passionately committed to you, to us, and to our growth together,
> for each other and for the sake of building friendship in the world . . .

I should probably confess at this point that the song 'What a friend we have in Jesus' has never done it for me, partly because the melody to which it is generally sung has an element of music hall about it, making the friendship sound twee and superficial, but also because the words seem to undermine the essentially mutual nature of friendship itself.

The lyrics make Jesus' role very clear. To summarize and paraphrase, it seems that he bears our sins and griefs, shares our sorrows, knows our every weakness and offers tea and sympathy when earthly friends are fickle. It's less clear what our own responsibilities in this relationship are. Our role seems somewhat passive and, dare I say it, needy. We simply hand over the uncomfortable package of sins and woes and walk away much uplifted. Problem solved. What a great friend.

Naturally there will be times when we are the passive and needy partner or the 'high-maintenance' one in a group of friends. But there's an essential ebb and flow in friendship, a give and take that ensures that the same person is not always giving and the other not always taking. So perhaps a more grown-up idea of friendship would be a better metaphor for our relationship with Jesus and with God.

Real friendship is complex, nuanced and reciprocal. It is based partly on fondness and familiarity, but also on respect and sometimes perhaps even reticence. Friendship can develop under all sorts of circumstances and for a wide variety of reasons. We make friends in adversity, in celebration, when we work with someone, play together or stand alongside each other at the school gate. We are attracted to people as friends because they are like us, or because they are not like us at all.

Friendship can be the essential thread that enables sexual relationships to continue to work over time. People who are part of a couple may do a considerable degree of socializing separately, may take up very different roles within the home, may work long hours and only manage to snatch brief amounts of time together during the week, may have forgotten how to 'date' one another, may even be wondering how it is that this relationship is so different from their original expectations – but at the end of the day, if they are still friends there is a decent chance that the rest can be recaptured or reinvented.

Someone who has been married previously said to me that in a new relationship she is discovering how it feels to be with a partner who is actually also her friend. 'There was none of that last time,' she said. Of course there is truth in the truism that maintaining a level of romance and mystique in long-term relationships will help to keep alive their sexual thrill, but without doubt friendship is also a powerful tool in sustaining partnerships.

True friendship can survive a lot. It can survive differences and prolonged silence, misunderstanding and lifestyle changes. It can even be built around these things. It requires tenacity and a desire to stay connected, but it does not demand that we see each other all the time. Some of the best friendships are those in which we can be out of touch for a very long period, but when we reconnect we still love and respect one another just as much as ever.

As a child I was quite comfortable with the idea that my friendship with Jesus was of the unchallenging kind, ever-gentle and rather one-sided, a sort of spiritual security hug. As an adult with a more knowing approach I can see in the Jesus of the Gospels the sort of friend who pulls no punches and rarely fails to see what I try to hide as well as what I'm willing to reveal. I find myself wondering what sort of friend he must have been to the disciples and the women with whom he spent time – elusive, strange, blunt, compassionate, obtuse, humorous, intense, fascinating. Our relationship with this rather less domesticated and more interesting God may well actually resonate with aspects of our human friendships.

In the past couple of years the habit of conducting friendships via the web has increased exponentially in popularity. For a long time I strongly resisted signing up to any of them, partly because everybody else was doing it and I got an adolescent kick out of refusing to comply, but more out of a sense that the internet lacks boundaries: people might somehow tread on my space, and the information I put out there could go where I would rather it did not.

Oddly enough those questions hit the news for the first time the week after I gave in and opened a Facebook account. And because they raise fundamental issues about how we relate to one another as human beings, the questions will not stop when the legalities are resolved. How much is it appropriate for us to disclose to one another? With how many people can we actually be intimate? How do we develop meaningful relationships using methods of communication that are not face to face?

These issues and many others manifest themselves as soon as we have signed up to Facebook or another such network. We have to decide whether our page is just for good friends, or do we want to use it to meet new people through friends, and friends of friends, and friends of friends of friends? What do we do about the people who ask to be our Facebook friend whose requests we want to turn down? Ignore them or flatly reject them? Which is the less hurtful option?

Using technology to expand our friendship network carries risks. It takes a mere slip of the finger to get us into territory we really hadn't intended to explore. There was the woman who sent an invitation to her entire address book, including all the parents of the Sunday School that she runs, asking them to be her Facebook friends. Then came the embarrassed follow-up message explaining what had happened, but reassuring everyone that they were very welcome to say 'yes' if they would like to be friends with her. She's a lovely woman: anyone would want to be her friend. Which is probably why she will now have to set up a new Facebook site under a pseudonym if she just wants to chat with her real mates.

We are, in real life, part of a web of human interconnections. Our stories can only be separated from other people's with great difficulty and editing. Internet socializing networks emphasize this fact by their very nature. Join them and you are part of a much bigger picture. Anything you say or do may reverberate elsewhere.

It seems to me that once we have negotiated these questions, these internet sites open up huge possibilities of positive networking and friendship while simultaneously being an exercise in walking on eggshells. There is tremendous potential for misunderstanding or upsetting people – not so different from how it is when we relate to people in the flesh, but somehow the arena is bigger and the potential to mess it up feels greater.

Addressing the idea of friendships that are fostered primarily through email, texts and internet sites, Mark Vernon warns us that 'screens screen' and 'there is no substitute for face time'.[2] We miss so much by not seeing one another's faces and body language or hearing the inflection in a voice. Instead we can be privy to such details as: 'I am going outside', 'I am wondering what to have for lunch', 'I am putting on my socks'. Why would anyone want to know?

I wonder too what such an experience as Second Life, another popular web-based pursuit, does to us. There we have the ability to exist as a different 'avatar', to be whoever we want to be. In daily life we can, of course, choose to withhold a good deal of information about ourselves, but it is much harder in the flesh to create an entirely different persona without anyone noticing! Second Life may be a way of not living your First Life. Or, more positively, it may give people the privacy and confidence they need to become something different in their First Life too.

All of this may remind us, as we reflect on the idea of 'God as friend', that any friendship requires us to have courage and sensitivity, openness to the unexpected, and to accept to some extent the invasion of our space. Perhaps the question of how much we choose to reveal is superfluous when it comes to our relationship with the God who made us, but we most of us foolishly attempt dishonesty with our Creator from time to time, and can assume far too easily that we have correctly second-guessed what God is thinking. If 'screens screen' then we can be sure that the veil between heaven and earth isn't entirely transparent either. And our inner life, exploring a relationship with God, somehow has to relate to our life in the world: there's nothing virtual about it; it shapes what we are in the here and now.

In his book *The Easter Stories*, Trevor Dennis looks at the biblical description of Eden and unfolds what the story might be saying about the relationship between Adam, Eve and God. He identifies the loss of an easy intimacy with God, of a relationship that seemed to be something remarkably like friendship, as the core meaning of the expulsion from the Garden. He speaks of the tragedy as being 'not just a loss of innocence, but a loss of intimacy, of that easy, natural, fearless relationship with a God who walks in his garden in the evening breeze, and whose sound is mysteriously audible to human ears'.[3]

To a certain extent all friendships, however conducted, make us vulnerable to misunderstanding, disappointment or even disapproval, just as they open up the potential for untold riches of encouragement, empathy, fun and exploration. This is partly because good friendship involves a delicate blend of intimacy and spaciousness, a balance we find in that brief but beautiful description in Genesis that hints at the intended nature of God's relationship with human beings.

As Dennis makes clear, all that we say about God is necessarily metaphor, allusion, likeness and approximation. No language can stretch to encompass God. It soon breaks down when we try to use the only terms we can – those of our own experience – to describe our Creator. But the story of Eden and the shift in the relationship between humanity and God is a myth that conveys the truth of unfulfilled potential – the potential of an intimate relationship with the Creator who gave us form, life and being.

Of course a relationship of intimacy with God will be of a different nature from one between two human beings physically present to one another and occupying the same space–time continuum. But Dennis' explorations say something profound about the possibility of God being in a more vulnerable relationship with us than we usually assume, and because of that vulnerability a relationship more intimate and close. He points us to three moments in the Hebrew scriptures when there seems to be a surprising familiarity and openness between God and a human being.

First, there is the story in Genesis 22 in which Jacob wrestles with God. Dennis points out that although it is ultimately Jacob who is wounded by the encounter, in fact there is a moment when God asks Jacob to let go – as though God can no longer bear the struggle. Second, in Exodus 33.11 Moses is said to speak face to face with God, 'as one speaks to a friend'. It blows our minds to think just exactly how that would work and how it would feel. The third, and perhaps most striking and evocative example, is that found in Exodus 32.11, where we find Moses tending to the Lord. Dennis gives us a literal translation of the Hebrew: 'And Moses soothed the face of the Lord his God'.[4]

There is something tremendously moving, though unfamiliar and a little disturbing, in this image of a vulnerable God asking to be released, talking with someone as a friend, being open to human soothing. It goes to the very heart of the Christian gospel, which in this light is seen as the hope that we can actually have a relationship with a Creator who 'speaks without any prior formality, allows us to hear what is going through his mind, walks to and fro so that [Adam and Eve] can hear him coming, engages them in dialogue and even becomes tailor and makes them clothes.'[5] Dennis concludes that the author of this passage in Genesis is saying to us, 'This is the intimacy with which we were made. This is the intimacy for which we were made.'[6]

There is something in this exploration of friendship with God that is very much about that blend of intimacy and space essential to good human friendships. Space is necessary if we are not to feel crushed or overwhelmed by other people. We need it in order to define where we end and they begin, because it is in that space that we can offer what we are without oppressing them and vice versa. But without intimacy, the sharing of our deepest thoughts and concerns and the willingness to make ourselves vulnerable, to admit to our imperfections and share our strengths, friendship does not develop other than at a very superficial level.

Of course the level of the friendship will dictate the level of intimacy and self-exposure. There is a fine line between helpful self-revelation and that which is just plain embarrassing for everyone. It's the difference between carefully revealing a tasteful bit of leg and brazenly flashing your cellulite. Similarly, honesty in friendships needs to be carefully applied. Doris Lessing once wrote that we should never destroy a person's picture of themselves – they may not have anything with which to replace it.[7] Considering this possibility before delivering a shaft of brutal honesty can be the wisest and most mature thing to do.

There is a place that speaks to me of both the isolation and interconnectedness of human beings and our need for both intimacy and space. The redeveloped St Pancras Station in London is an architectural phenomenon. In its Victorian heyday it was known as 'the cathedral of the railways'. Those at the heart of the regeneration project hoped that this cavernous space would not only be a starting point and a terminus for people's journeys, but somewhere to relax and kick back with friends. People would visit the longest champagne bar in Europe, browse in the shops and watch the world arrive and depart, observing the countless actions and reactions of human intercourse.

At the opening ceremony, Her Majesty the Queen referred to St Pancras as 'not just a station but a destination', a place dedicated to journeys and to relationships, much cited as a tool for bringing London into greater proximity with mainland Europe. 'Now Sheffield is closer to Paris', said the Queen, 'and Nottingham closer to Brussels.' Arguably, being 20 minutes closer to Paris has not on its own enabled a greater understanding of our European neighbours. It requires more than proximity to build friendship – but proximity is a start.

A sculpture of a man and a woman embracing graces St Pancras. They have been brought together, presumably, at their journeys' end. Two individuals have successfully found one another, in this vast space that gives us in equal measure the potential both to be lost and to be found.

Friendship is a way of not being alone in the world; of having somewhere to go and someone to meet. Good friendship requires both space and intimacy, the willingness to be vulnerable and the ability to be strong for the other. Friendship of the most life-building sort, within which we can be wholly open and exploratory and creative, encourages us to be the best that we can be – 'For each other and for the sake of building friendship in the world'.

Most of us would probably recognize from one context or another that if people who need to work on something together can meet as human beings over a glass of wine, cup of coffee or meal, far more can be achieved and sometimes more quickly than via more formal methods. There are fewer misunderstandings, better business decisions, more creative and exciting projects dreamed up, and life is more enjoyable and rewarding. The building of relationships, 'friendship for the sake of the world', creates space and flexibility, and releases good and constructive hormones.

Of course the more our time is filled with work and the domestic essentials, the harder we find it to carve out the necessary commitment for significant friendships. But it is always worth it. Our relationships with other individuals are invaluable both in themselves but also for what is enabled in their hinterlands. Perhaps this is where networking comes into its own with the multitudinous connections it can forge. The reverberations of friendship can be a significant force for good.

Michael Sandle's vast 2007 charcoal drawing, *Iraq triptych*, rather ruthlessly depicts Tony and Cherie Blair standing naked outside the door of 10 Downing Street, an image deliberately evocative of Adam and Eve banished from Eden. The Blairs are flanked by scenes from the 2003 Iraq war, and the clear message is that the consequences of Mr Blair's political decisions have been exposed – the couple are naked before everyone and desperately in need of friendship.

If friendship is in fact an appropriate metaphor to use of our relationship with God, then that friendship is characterized from God's side by breathtaking grace – the kind of grace we see in a Creator whose artistic approach in sketching out our lives is infinitely sympathetic, and who has no desire to see us with our backs against the wall but rather encourages us, as a friend, beyond Eden, drawing the subtle patterns and intricate possibilities of our lives with spaciousness and mercy.

Real friendship reflects our relationship with a God whom we experience to be constant, sometimes; the quintessential good sounding-board (maybe the writer of 'What a friend we have in Jesus' was simply saying that), who is also energizing, tantalizing and something of a challenge at times; the God whom we love and admire but can't actually pin down, who as well as being above and beyond us, in some sense occupies the same space we do yet does not intrude but meets with us in vulnerability and openness; a God whom we can fight yet survive fighting, and who may actually be disturbed by the experience of wrestling with us; a God whose face we may tentatively and with awe want to soothe when we see what is happening to some parts of creation.

There is something disturbing about the possibility of intimate friendship with a God who might ask to be released from our wrestling hold or whose brow we might wipe. This God is a far cry from the impassive and self-contained Alpha-male deity who, for a multitude of reasons to do with our guilt and anger and a lack of alternative images, lurks in the corners of our consciousness. God as grown-up friend is a far riskier metaphor and predicates a more precarious relationship.

But we may find this God to be more real than the other version, as we take hesitant steps towards the space and intimacy that characterize any truthful relationship. We may relish the space that we are given in this grown-up way of relating. We may find ourselves drawn to this risky enterprise of intimacy with

God because of all that we might learn and experience. We may decide to take that risk to discover how it might change us and what it might do to our understanding of ourselves. We might take the risk for ourselves, 'For each other and for the sake of building friendship in the world'.

4

July: bringing it all to the party
Public space and hinterlands

——◆◆◆——

In July 2008 I found myself in a dilemma. I'd been invited to a three-day conference on leadership, to be attended by the women bishops of the Anglican Communion and a number of female clergy from the Church of England. I very much wanted to go, but Joseph was nine weeks old and I could only get there if I took him along. My dilemma was this: would turning up with a baby be perceived as an acceptable, even a radical thing to do – or would I just look like that incompetent woman who can't manage her childcare?

So I emailed a colleague to ask what she thought, and she replied with some passion: 'Bring the baby. It reminds us all (even the non-mothers like me) that women are trying to do things differently, that we *are* different and that we do have a different hinterland from our male colleagues.'

Male or female, we all have a hinterland. It is made up of the people we love, the work that we do, the stuff that gets us out of bed in the morning, our worries about money, our concerns about health and the many other things that make us who we are. Whether we are introvert, extrovert or a mixture of both, whatever makes us cry, whoever makes us laugh and however we spend our time, we each bring something particular to the party. That is our hinterland.

To talk about men and women having a different hinterland because of their gender is immediately to raise hackles and a whole raft of questions. People hold widely divergent views on whether the genders fundamentally differ and if so in what way, let alone on what the implications of those differences might be for our public and private lives.

Many women of my generation would say that we have been formed and educated in the same way as men. Some of us are wary of gender generalizations. Every time I begin a sentence with 'Women tend to . . .' or 'Women are better at . . .', I want to add the disclaimer that there are men like that too. Yet I'm often drawn back to the thought that a room full of women feels different from a room full of men, which feels different from a room full of men and women. And I remember the meetings I've taken part in where I've been momentarily paralysed by the realization that I was the only woman present.

Whatever we think about all of this we may well agree that the arrival of women in 'public space' has raised significant questions for both genders. So if you consider all this politicized talk about women to be outdated or irrelevant to you, bear with me for a while, for under the layers of rhetoric and gender jargon, beyond the habit of boxing people in and some rather too easy talk of inclusion, there may be important issues that affect us all. These are to do with our hinterlands and how we negotiate the relationship between public and domestic space. As these are questions about how we explore our full humanity we might also, in the process of exploring them, learn something about God.

Of course there have always been women who have occupied public space, but for much of history they have been the exceptions. For centuries the lives of most were lived almost wholly in the domestic sphere. Their experience of building and shaping community, taking initiative and exercising leadership was primarily in that context.

Even now in the UK, in the majority of partnerships where there are children or parents who are dependants, it is the woman who will be the main caregiver. In most occupations women are over-represented among the part-time workers and under-represented in the senior roles. A *Sunday Telegraph* list of April 2008 of the 100 most powerful people in British culture included only 18 women, just three of whom made it into the top 20.[1] That same month, 68 per cent of employers said that they would like the right to ask a woman about her childcare arrangements when interviewing her for a job.[2]

I am not saying that this is simply 'what has been done to women'. Women have made choices in relation to the focus of their lives and still do. Writing in *The Guardian* in June 2008, Baroness Lola Young, a life peer, acknowledged the possibility that if the House of Lords became an entirely elected assembly, the number of female peers would reduce because women are much less likely to put themselves forward.[3] Not so long ago the same issue was identified in the Church, though there is some recent evidence that women are very much up for taking on senior roles, provided there is room to shape those roles according to their particular insights and perspectives.

So it seems that it is still pioneering for a woman to take authority in a public context. On the occasion of her electoral defeat, Hillary Clinton said that she may not have won the campaign but that that 'highest, hardest, glass ceiling' now had 'about 18 million cracks in it'.[4]

With all this in mind when my colleague said 'bring the baby to the conference', she was effectively saying: bring your domestic stuff to this public event because it reminds us that we all have our equivalent of that, and we all bring more to the party than just our public persona.

Both men and women know the truth of this: that our lives are not two-dimensional but many-faceted. Yet there is a disjunction between what we know and how we actually behave. We may accept in theory that what and who we are in one sphere of life is intricately connected with what and who we are in every other, but we have a strong tendency to try to keep things separate, and perhaps particularly to keep home invisible when we are at work. When someone goes against this trend we can find ourselves surprisingly indignant, whether it is the member of our team who always seems to be asking for favours because of personal circumstances, or someone in a prominent role who chooses to put family first.

In 2007 David Miliband, the British Foreign Secretary, made a very public decision to take two weeks' paternity leave during the state visit of King Abdullah of Saudi Arabia, and to absent himself from a keynote conference involving the two nations. His decision was highly controversial. Some people thought it was outrageous that he should step back from his public role just because he and his wife had had a baby. They argued that the role of Foreign Secretary being one of the biggest jobs in government, it is not a remit that can be set aside for private concerns. But others felt that it was no bad thing for a senior politician to be seen trying to juggle work and domesticity just like the rest of us. They thought that the decision humanized Miliband in his senior role, and that that was no bad thing.

I have no idea what I would have done had I been in the Foreign Secretary's position. But his dilemma was an example, writ large, of the sort we all face when we ask ourselves, 'How can I occupy both the public and domestic spheres while maintaining my integrity and my sanity and not letting people down?'

Shortly after the conference of Anglican women leaders that Joseph and I attended, I listened to a debate on BBC Radio 4's *Woman's Hour*. It was about the impact on the devolved national assemblies of the UK of an increase in the number of female politicians. One of the observations made was that it isn't just the working environment of the Parliaments that has changed, but the policies that are brought forward for debate. I missed the bit that told us what those new policies might be about, but the implication seems to be that there are areas of life now explored by politicians that would have remained untouched by public debate had the group of people for whom those issues are pressing not themselves moved into politics.

Put like this it sounds so obvious that it would and should be so, but there has been such a long tradition of the separation of public and private that we naturally shy away from bringing our personal and domestic experience into the wider arena. For women this is often because we fear being considered unprofessional. We might be sidelined as someone whose job is apparently not their main priority and who therefore need not be taken entirely seriously. One commentator suggests that feminism has shot women in the foot by its singular focus on equal access to the workplace rather than presenting a diversity of women's experiences as being equally valid:

> An equality founded on . . . public significance has produced an emphasis on work as the only measure of parity. Motherhood, as it is lived, is still individual, personal, private, and therefore deeply undervalued, sometimes even by those of us . . . who move between the 'real' world of work and the shadow world of family life.[5]

It is hard to believe that this total separation of our private and working lives is the best way to become a fully functioning, healthily rounded human being. Surely there are things that we learn in each area of our experience that are pertinent elsewhere? Many employers have begun to recognize that there are, and to encourage employees, at least in times of economic stability, to have interests and commitments outside of work or even through work that don't necessarily relate directly to their job remits. And employers willing to invest in their employees recognize the pressures of juggling home and work, and try to have a degree of flexibility and sympathy when people are dealing with major issues in their private lives.

Of course there are times when we have to make hard calls about priorities: deadlines at work clashing with illness at home; pressure to put in long hours when what we actually need is time away from the relentlessness of achieving and producing and completing. There are times when it is inappropriate for the domestic agenda to impinge on work: we may have to be fully functioning to the best of our ability in spite of the fact that we are going through a very difficult stage in our relationship or are worried about the health of an ageing parent.

And there are people whose careers inevitably involve significant amounts of time away from home and family. In early 2007, Faye Turney's story hit the UK news with some force. The 25-year-old sailor was taken hostage when the Royal Navy ship on which she was serving allegedly strayed into Iranian waters. In spite of ourselves, many of us were shocked to learn that Turney was on active service while being the parent of a young child. I say in spite of ourselves, because we have always known that this is a common situation for men in a similar position.

In an interview just prior to her abduction, Turney referred to the split in her life between two distinct and radically different arenas:

> I really do love my job, but I love my daughter also. If I didn't love my job I wouldn't be able to do it, but if I had to make a choice my daughter would win every time – without a shadow of a doubt, no question about it.[6]

With a wry smile a friend tells a very different story on the theme of balancing career against the needs of home. As an actor she sometimes works on location for several weeks at a time, and in a bid to find a new solution to the issue of childcare she interviewed for an au pair. Mindful of that much-smirked-about dilemma faced by anyone with an attractive partner who engages a younger woman to help out with their children, she carefully employed a girl who, the evidence suggested, was unconcerned by considerations such as weight, wardrobe and facial hair – only to discover on her return several weeks later that the au pair had slimmed down dramatically, hit Oxford Street with a vengeance and even had her belly button pierced!

The relationship between our domestic and public lives is complex. It can play on our insecurities and absorb huge amounts of energy in managing the boundaries. For people such as Faye Turney it even involves significant calculated risks. However, a creative conversation between work, home and all other aspects of our lives can be as rewarding as it is sometimes exhausting. The gains lie not just in what we might experience as individuals but in what we as communities, institutions, families and friends can learn if we call on the breadth of experience within ourselves and between one another in our exploration of what it means to live a full human life.

Apparently there is a Central African tribe where it is the women who go out to hunt at night. If there are newborn babies then of course they will wake up at some point when their mothers are away. Those of us brought up to assume that a very small baby who cries in the night should be fed will feel a sense of anxiety about this, but there is a solution: the fathers suckle the babies. There's no milk involved but it works. The babies are satisfied simply by the action of sucking. Some of our most basic assumptions about what is normative are challenged by the experiences of other people.

We need to be careful, however, not to replace one set of assumptions with another. There is a danger of this in relation to the debate around whether or not there is such a thing as a masculine and a feminine leadership style. There was a time when the version of this conversation within the Church seemed to be heading for the conclusion that women are more collaborative or 'circular' in their approach to leadership and men more hierarchical.

I have doubts about this even as a generalization. I suspect that all we can say at the present is that there are different models, styles and approaches to leadership, that no one should feel constrained by a particular gender stereotype, and that as women leaders become more numerous at all levels in all organizations, yet more possible models of leadership will be added to the resources available to us already.

Susan Durber, in her book *Preaching Like a Woman*, argues that 'to be embodied as a woman makes a difference to how you know and how you are known . . . and how you talk about faith'. She suggests that the presence of women in the pulpit indicates that preaching can no longer focus on 'one kind of human experience as though it were normative'.[7]

When I was on the clergy staff team at St Martin-in-the-Fields, my colleague David Monteith and I competed to mention things in sermons that were not generally alluded to from the pulpit. I think I won definitively one Sunday with a reference to ovaries. This was part of our general approach to a life lived with reference to God, believing as we did (and still do) that God is inextricably involved with all that we are and not just some of it.

There is something about cultivating the ability to bring the whole of our self into the present moment in the place in which we happen to be. It makes it more possible for us to make sensible and appropriate decisions about which aspects of ourselves and our experience we reveal in the context.

At a public lecture facilitated by an organization called Women of the Year, I watched the singer–songwriter Joan Armatrading fulfil her role as president. I think she was the most delightful example I have ever seen of someone at ease with herself and her role. Not for her the fashionably heeled 'woman with a public persona' look. She strolled her easy way on to the stage in laid-back mode, wearing comfortable clothes and trainer-style shoes and one of the warmest smiles I've ever seen in a lecture hall.

She appeared to be fully herself, fabulously able to make a personal connection with the audience, free of any sense of role playing, quite simply enjoying the moment. There was something about her that suggested she is one of those people essentially just the same wherever she is. I couldn't imagine her having a crisis about how much of her private self to bring to the public party.

It occurs to me that if any of us is to feel fully included in the Church, we need to know that we can come as we are and risk bringing everything that we are with us. We know that before God we are, quite simply and non-negotiably, naked. We are who we are and we know that there is nothing we can do to hide anything. This is why it concerns me that the Church in some times and places seems wary of welcoming us with all our baggage. Of course that is a sweeping statement and an oversimplification, but it does seem that we have often capitulated, perhaps unwittingly, to the idea that we should leave a lot of what we are outside the door when we enter 'sacred space'. We have been tempted to abandon some of our uncertainties, our physicality, perhaps our sexuality – the stuff of our life that we somehow consider to be less than holy because it jars with the sometimes sanitized atmosphere of church.

There's a passage in Barack Obama's book, *The Audacity of Hope*, in which he is talking about his early experience of the black American church. The picture is refreshingly different to the one I've just painted of other churches:

> In the black community, the lines between sinner and saved were more fluid; the sins of those who came to church were not so different from the sins of those who didn't, and so were as likely to be talked about with humour as with condemnation. You needed to come to church precisely because you were of this world, not apart from it . . . because you were human and needed an ally in your difficult journey, to make the peaks and valleys smooth and render all those crooked paths straight.[8]

We believe that God's grace embraces us as we are, yet we can seem to work hardest at hiding our real selves when we are in the company of other people who believe that same thing. Of course this is not always true, but it sometimes is, and it means that we waste a fair amount of energy and miss a lot of opportunities to learn from one another. It is often in vulnerability and openness that we gain the greatest wisdom about the glorious complexity of ourselves and others, but that willingness to be vulnerable can only emerge when people trust each other enough to be real and bring the depths of their whole selves to the relationship or community. Doing so can be a gift to the whole church because it frees other people to do the same and opens the way for a greater honesty with ourselves and with God.

In the same way that there are hard decisions to be made about how to manage the relationship between our private lives and work, there will be issues around just how helpful it is in any given situation to wear our heart on our sleeve, say when people are relying on us to be the one who holds things together and hard decisions need to be taken. It is possible to be unhelpfully self-revealing, but nevertheless there will be many times when it is better to be open and vulnerable than defensive and closed.

So the presence of women in public space has raised issues that are just as pertinent to men, such as how we might relax the boundaries between different areas of our lives in order to live with greater integrity and wholeness; how we might encourage creative synergies between these different areas; how we can ensure that the experience and insights of all groups are taken seriously in the workplace, in the community and in all public contexts. In a sense there is no such thing as a normative experience – our different hinterlands, perspectives and combinations of roles and commitments ensure that human interaction is more complex and rich than that.

Bringing all that we are to the party and ensuring that everyone has the chance to do the same, we can make connections between the different aspects of our own experience and discover resonances between ours and other people's. In all of this we want to discover the things about God that we are in danger of missing unless everybody has the chance to bring their experiences to the public arena.

As we learn to do this more deliberately and with greater self-awareness, we begin to know more profoundly what it means to be made in God's image. The whole of ourself is part of this process: our gifts, weaknesses, gender-related experiences, hinterland and hormones, concerns and passions. We need to honour our own hinterland and embrace other people's, bringing our experience from our private and public lives as we unwrap the sacred in one another's experiences as well as in our own.

5

August: the Maria von Trapp of Marylebone
Real life and God's agenda

One morning in mid-August I was half-listening to a radio interview with John Major. He was warning that diverting Heritage Lottery Funding from grassroots sports projects would jeopardize Britain's chances at the 2012 Olympics. The money was allegedly being used instead to meet targets relating to health, education and transport issues.

The journalist pointed out that some people might consider these matters more important than the assurance of sporting success. Sir John's enthused reply was something like: 'Well, those people are a bit sad, aren't they? Look at all the euphoria up and down this land at our successes in Beijing.'

The conversation revealed a very basic human dilemma. Lots of things are important and they are important in entirely different ways. The triumph of an athlete, the fulfilment of his or her God-given physical talent and potential, can't be measured with any degree of parity against the need to address the problems of our phenomenally overstrained National Health Service. Yet they are realities that exist in the same world. The tensions are sometimes direct, sometimes oblique. But all of the issues are real.

This connects with a question that periodically gets under my skin: 'Where is real life to be found?' We make daily, complex, nuanced decisions about where to put our energy and time, our money and passion – where to pay attention. That is what shapes our life to be what it is. But are we choosing real life, the stuff that is actually important, or are we frittering away our time and resources?

We can only explore all of this from the context of our own lives. I'm 41 and married, with three children aged seven, four and one. My first real job was working for a firm of solicitors in Lancashire, advising people on immigration issues. Then 13 years ago I was ordained as an Anglican priest in the Church of England, a different sort of reality but no less real. After ordination I worked in a parish in Lancaster for two years, then spent eight years on the team at St Martin-in-the-Fields in Trafalgar Square.

I left St Martin's when our eldest daughter started school and I decided not to take on a parish of my own because juggling that particular role with vocations to marriage and parenting felt just a little too precarious. Many men and women do it, of course, and very creatively. Countless people combine very full-on jobs with bringing up young children. Whether through choice or necessity that is their reality. But it felt as though I was being prompted in a different direction, to be partly a stay-at-home parent and partly something else. Again, a path that quite a number of women find themselves taking.

So for the past three years I've been trying to work out what it might mean to be a portfolio priest or perhaps a priest without portfolio. I split my time between doing some writing and radio broadcasting and being trustee of a couple of church-related organizations and chair of governors of a Church of England secondary school. My day-job is to work on issues relating to female clergy both in London and nationally. And as a consequence of all of this we have complicated childcare arrangements that often make me think it might have been simpler to have one very full-time job after all! But that's almost certainly an illusion of the grass-is-always-greener variety.

For a while I struggled to find one phrase that sums up 'what I do', until Layla, the five-year-old daughter of a friend, while watching *The Sound of Music* one day pointed at Julie Andrews and said to her mum, 'That's what Hannah's and Olivia's mum is.' Since then I've had a vague and rather levelling image of myself as the Maria von Trapp of Marylebone (or of Edgware Road, but that doesn't sound so glamorous or alliterate so well).

Each of us works at finding our place in life and what we are supposed to do with it. To achieve this we need to find a way of prioritizing our attention, and we do it according to our life experience and the information before us at the time. Jesus did the same. No one accuses him of not fulfilling his brief because he failed to broker peace between the Jews and the Samaritans. He did what he could in the time available, with the bits of reality that were thrown into the melting pot of his life, the individuals he met and the opportunities he crafted.

For many of us our daily dilemmas involve juggling the needs of children or partner with professional commitments. This might mean managing our own health against the background of a punishing pace at work, or balancing the care of elderly relatives with the necessity to preserve our own space and sanity. There are endless variations, but in all of this we ask: am I supposed to be here or there, giving myself to these issues or those, committed to that cause or this, these people or those?

These are tough calls written into the very fabric of life. They can only be dealt with one by one, in trepidation, weighing the issues and the impact on other people with loving precision. We all get it right sometimes and wrong sometimes, and we spend a lifetime making adjustments – sometimes small, sometimes significant – as we feel ourselves being driven towards certain priorities or away from others.

They are also issues that can put a huge strain on relationships. However committed we are to each other's happiness, development and even freedom, the fact is that if you live with someone there are lots of times when your decisions about work impact directly on that person. One small instance at a time seems manageable, but the cumulative effect of just one more late night followed by one more early morning followed by one more plea to do the shopping or school run when it isn't your turn can cause a level of resentment that surprises even the person who's feeling it. It's such a tediously platitudinous thing to say, but the fact is that both people have to make compromises, even if it means risking the annoyance or disappointment of colleagues. A relationship just can't sustain two people always doing everything that they want to regardless of the other.

In this context, and many others, there will be times when we feel free in the decisions we make and other times when we are more constrained, whether that is by our loyalty to certain people, the responsibilities we have been given or taken on, or our emotional or financial limitations. It can be exhilarating making all these decisions, or it can be exhausting. It involves a lot of uncertainty, but always it is about engaging with real life.

So like most people I juggle my work responsibilities (and within that, in my case, one set of work responsibilities with another) with my commitment to family, friends and relatives. I'm learning how to be part of the community at the school gate and I'm discovering what it is to be a member of a congregation on the other side of the altar, in the pew not the pulpit, failing to keep my children quiet during the intercessions. When people ask me, 'When did you get your vocation?' I want to ask them, 'Which one? Lawyer – about 20 years ago. Wife – 1999. Mother – more recently, and then again, and again. Oh, but you mean priest?!'

Juggling vocations or priorities is for most people the day-to-day stuff of life. And often it will involve a degree of guilt and the sense of never quite managing to be all that we need to be. A lot of us think we spend too much time working; some of us would give anything to be able to but for whatever reason find ourselves without enough work. We all feel that the clock of our lives is ticking and we know that those minutes won't be given back. So we want to get these decisions about our priorities right – and to do this by working out what is on God's agenda both for us and for the world.

One of the marked differences in my life since I left parish ministry is that I am no longer surrounded by people who chat with me on a daily basis about the church's mission priorities, the theology of last Sunday's sermon or what God might be saying to us about Zimbabwe. No longer can I walk into a meeting and expect to see on the agenda what someone thinks God is concerned with today. I have to work that out for myself, in the grit and the glory of everyday life outside of the structures of the institution. If I am trying to uncover the life within the life of the world, where should I start?

I live in London and get a vicarious buzz from glimpsing the life of such power-centres as the Houses of Parliament, Whitehall, the Royal Courts of Justice and countless other national institutions. It's tempting to see all that as the real 'real life', the vital stuff, the life of the movers and shakers that shapes the life of the nation. Londoners are accused of living on an island. And of course to us, in our less observant moments, it does seem that everything important, nation-forming, potentially world-influencing, happens here.

But is real life to be found only in the political arena, in boardrooms and cathedrals, think-tanks and senior management teams? Is it not, rather, in the places where human life is shaped by the decisions of medics, social workers, teachers, human-rights lawyers and probation officers? Could it be in the concerns and contributions of smaller communities and rural life, rather than the life of the cities? Or again, is it in the playground and the school run? Where is the really important stuff of life to be found?

To this there is a related question. When people anguish about their work–life balance, do they say they want more time at home because home represents in some sense the most authentic part of our lives, or is it the opposite, that they return to work after a career break or even a fortnight's leave and quietly suspect that's real life, and what they've just experienced was a brief interlude?

Most days I come to the conclusion that real life is quite simply to be found where we are, among those God has given us to love, completing the tasks we find ourselves having the responsibility for, being the son, daughter, brother, aunt, friend, colleague, adviser, confidante that we happen to be. That is the agenda God has for us, and whatever it is, that's what counts.

We struggle, of course, with our desire to be the man or woman next door whose life seems so ordered or the person in the workplace whose career trajectory is so much the one we want for ourselves. We catch ourselves wanting to inhabit the lives of our heroes, roll back the years and relive them in order to pack in more activity and achievements, be the one who changed the direction of our organization or be able to influence events on a bigger stage than our own.

Trying to be somebody else is fruitless, but perhaps there's a connection sometimes between how we present ourselves – even quite literally what we choose to wear and how it makes us feel – and what we become. The Archdeacon of Charing Cross recently confessed to me that he has been moonlighting as an assistant to television celebs Trinny Woodall and Susannah Constantine. His role related specifically to the episode 'Country Ladies' in the ITV series *Trinny and Susannah Meet their Match*, in which the fashion gurus attempted to transform the appearance of a country GP, a mayor, a vicar, a bellringer and a Sunday School teacher.

The Archdeacon's sartorial taste being impeccable, he joined the panel of advisors who worked with the infamous pair, and was witness to, perhaps instrumental in, some miraculous transformations. The contrast between how some of the women spoke about themselves at the beginning and at the end of the process was almost miraculous. In particular one floral-clad lady who was deeply disapproving of the amount of cleavage Susannah is wont to flaunt was extremely womanly in her new incarnation (all without baring anything but her soul). It was wonderful to watch, and made me think that actually these matters are not superficial. How we present ourselves can be about how we see ourselves now or what we might hope to become.

Real life is wherever we are set, being writ large by ourselves and those we share it with. Craving a bigger stage is absurd, unless that really is what our gifts are most suited to. But wherever we stand and whatever our part, perhaps it helps to have a clear picture of the part we think we are both called to play and to forge for ourselves, and of how we need to think and act and present ourselves to the world in order to do it most effectively. In any case, whether our stage is big or small we rarely know what direction the action is going to take next.

In Hanif Kureishi's novel *Something to Tell You*, the narrator observes: 'I've seen many bad shows, but some of them had great intervals.'[1] Some of our richest experiences are gained in the intervals between what we consider to be the real action.

On a different though related theme, it's often said that God's timing is perfect. I would dispute that, because I know from experience that it can be dreadful. God lobs things into the melting pot of my life at the most awkward of times. Opportunities to do something new, to move on, to embrace another steep learning curve generally come to me at the worst of moments. I was eight months pregnant and trying to get two young children showered at arms' length after their swimming lesson, without either getting shampoo in their eyes or drenching myself, when my mobile rang and I foolishly answered it. 'Is it a good time to talk?' asked my former boss. 'No,' I said, 'but the whole of my life is like this, so go ahead.' 'Would you consider being chair of governors of a secondary school?' he asked. 'Love to,' I heard myself reply, ignoring my lack of relevant knowledge and skills, the need to find childcare for the imminently due baby, and the well-known wisdom that being a school governor takes over your life. So no, God's timing is terrible, but sometimes it's still right to say 'yes', because it's a pure, unexplored, goldmine of reality that's on offer.

On the other hand, I do ask myself fairly frequently whether living life quite so utterly to the full is sustainable. The trick of not overfilling it is one I still have not learnt. Many of us pack our lives with so much activity that we have little energy to enjoy fully the good things, and find ourselves unable to relax even when the opportunity is there. When a friend I hadn't seen for a while asked me recently how life is these days, I found myself saying guiltily, 'It's almost unmanageably full. It's mostly good stuff but there's just too much of it.' And of course it isn't all good and easy. There's the friend who's seriously ill, the relative who's long-term clinically depressed, the anniversary of a miscarried baby and the elusive nature of my self-confidence that can be insidiously undermining. But I do admit to having days when it can feel quite overwhelming to juggle it all – privileged, but overwhelming nevertheless.

There is also the issue of church, which is not life or death but definitely is a struggle. It may sound feeble, but when you have young children who would often rather go to the park, a baby who wants to join in with the service loudly and indiscriminately and a partner who isn't averse to church but never signed up to spending half of every weekend there, Sundays are problematic. They cut right across the limited downtime that modern families, couples and friends have together, and the culture of church is not always accessible to the entire range of needs represented in any one family, of which ours is hardly untypical. The Sabbath can, quite simply, get pretty stressful.

I know I am not alone in this because I talk to other people who would like their lives to connect more with the life of the church, but who struggle to do church at weekends too. So I find myself asking what different ways there might be of 'being church'. Then I wonder whether I should be seeking the local Anglican church's blessing to experiment with a 'different way'. But I soon realize that that puts me back at square one, which was the point at which I decided that being a vicar, nurturing a local worshipping community, simply doesn't meld with all my other commitments and vocations right now.

So for now I continue to try to introduce the children to the idea of a worshipping community, a place that takes spirituality seriously and expresses something of the hospitality of God, by attending – when we can – a number of different churches that suit our different needs. The one the girls prefer at the moment has buzzy children's activities, a hospitable approach to babies and takes the idea of community seriously. On the flip side, there are some fairly radical differences between my own understanding of God and that of the church in question, but for now that's fine, because the friendliness and warmth of the people who worship there make it a good place to be – as do the coffee and the bacon sandwiches on offer before the service begins.

Real life is found everywhere. So to return to where we began and the question of the importance of sport, it was difficult to watch much television in August 2008 without tuning in to the Beijing Olympics and getting caught up in the euphoria John Major referred to in that radio interview. Three gold medals for the cyclist Chris Hoy and one for Nicole Cooke in the road race, another for Ben Ainslie in the sailing, Christine Ohuruogu winning the 400 metres, and the gold for Rebecca Adlington that won her a pair of Manolo shoes back home – with 16 gold medals the British team had their best Olympics for a century.

Yet the entire hinterland of the games was fraught with political tension. The displacement of Beijing residents, China's human-rights record, the question of independence for Tibet and the attempt to circumscribe the activities of overseas journalists all became issues that dominated the news as much as the sporting events themselves. There was an inevitability about this, because they are very real issues, some of them life and death.

The question of how exactly the engagement between sport and politics should be handled is controversial, but the fact is that they exist not in two separate vacuums but as part of the same reality, that of the incredibly complex arena in which we live out our lives. What is global merges with what is local, what is political is also personal, and what we do and think in one area of our life has an impact on what we are in another.

In our own real lives – at home, at work, in the street, the community, the classroom, the office, the gym, the café; with friends, strangers, family, colleagues; yesterday, today and always – we are all dealing with what is on God's agenda. There is nothing more important than what is set before us, and all of it is real.

So we try to live it all fully, honestly, and in some sense with a light touch, taking what is on offer, recognizing that we cannot have everything all at once, embracing the riches that we have been given and trying to hold on to the hope of God's presence in the tragedies and the bits we find it hard to bear. We try to live it knowing that wherever we are and whatever we are doing, we cannot live anybody else's real life but only our own, for that is the one that makes us whoever we are and puts us wherever we are, gloriously unique in God's image, reflecting the divine love as nobody else can.

6

September: the woman in my godmother's clothes
Mid-life, fragility and meaning

❖

The woman in my godmother's clothes looks familiar but different. Somewhere in there is the person I know, but at the moment she cannot reach out and I cannot reach her. She looks as though she needs rescuing, but paradoxically she has withdrawn herself so far that no one but the person inside can initiate the rescue. For some time now she has been unable to do this. All we can do is wait, and still be here when it happens.

Statistics about mental health are far more rigorously recorded and publicized than ever before. Therefore we know that we have a one in eight chance of suffering at some time in our life from a mental health issue requiring treatment. The figure increases to one in four if we include those conditions that eventually mend themselves, but are no less real. I do not write with any authority on this issue, but I was a parish priest for a decade, and people talk to priests about these things. And then there are the stories told by friends and family.

Living with a mental health issue can be a full-time preoccupation. If it is the sort of illness that recurs then the sufferer is always aware, even in the good times, that there is a probability that it will come back. If it is an isolated episode of the kind that used to be commonly referred to as a 'nervous breakdown', it can take some years for a person to recover fully, if such a recovery is possible.

The brain of a human being is very malleable. Every interaction with the world influences the development of the neural pathways that connect our brain cells to each other. No two people have an identical brain because no two people have precisely the same interactions with the world around them, nor the same experiences or relationships. I got this from a lecture I attended by the neuroscientist Baroness Susan Greenfield, who explained that there is an increase in neural connections for so long as the brain remains active and healthy. Dementia is the result of those connections starting to atrophy and decrease, so that people have less and less ability to make sense of anything in relation to anything else. And they are then unable to find meaning in their lives as nothing connects to anything else any more.

Depression must be distinguished from dementia, of course. They are different conditions and one does not lead to the other. But I wonder whether, just as dementia leaves people struggling to find meaning, depression might sometimes have a similar effect. Either way, it seems that the ability to find meaning in our lives has an impact on our mental health. Or the other way round: mental ill health, which has many causes, some environmental and some chemical, can affect our ability to find meaning.

We spent a week in Northumberland in the summer, and on the last night of the holiday, walking back with her dad from a rock-pooling expedition on the beach, our daughter Hannah asked him what crabs are for. He negotiated his way through some sort of an answer that involved a reference to how life evolves, and then she asked 'So what's life for?'

It's quite shocking to hear that from a child because the question carries the resonances of existential angst, the threat of emptiness and of an echoing silence the length of ages. Many have asked what life is for out of sadness and incomprehension, because they're dealing with a loss of meaning in their own. We expect to find meaning in our work, our relationships and the general trajectory of our development. At times when we don't, things feel pretty bleak or at least a bit odd, disjointed, unhinged even. Most people want some sort of an answer to the question of what life is for, and many hope to discover a framework or some sort of reference point outside of themselves that confirms that it is for something worthwhile.

When people went to Jesus asking for healing and forgiveness they also came looking for meaning. They looked to him to make sense of their lives. And he told people what to do to access that meaning. He knew that Zacchaeus[1] could only live a meaningful life if he paid back what he owed, and that the rich young ruler must give away his wealth in order to discover what his life was really about.[2] On one occasion he told Mary that she had chosen the better part, to sit at his feet and learn about the heart of things;[3] on another it was her sister Mary from whom he drew out the meaning of his own life: 'You are the Messiah.'[4]

He dealt in meaning because that is what human beings want and need. He offered us our identity as children of God, marked, held, accounted for and infinitely loved. He gave us the hope of wholeness in our relationships with ourselves, with one another and with him; that is, with God. His invaluable legacy to us was the truth that each of us is a child of God – infinitely crafted, intimately embraced, filled with God's glory, shaped in God's image – and that that is our meaning.

But he also understood that for us meaning has to be concrete and worked out in the flesh. It is not enough for us to know that we are shaped in God's image. We have to test what shape that is, how it moulds our lives, what being a child of God makes of us and what we make of it. Jesus helped those who came to him to do this. He did it by touching their lives, telling them stories and asking them to take a long hard look at the world and themselves and to get on and change both.

In his wonderfully titled book, *Affluenza*, the psychotherapist Oliver James argues that we need just four things in order to be happy: to feel emotionally and materially secure; to be part of a community in which we give and receive; to feel effective in the tasks that we choose to do; and to feel autonomous and authentic, in charge of our own destiny and not hiding behind a mask.[5] If these are the components of a contented and meaningful life then surely they're a good starting point when we're looking for the sacred, for that which brings all things into being, makes all things tick, sustains the life of the world and gives us meaning.

As her parents we felt very challenged by Hannah's question because what if the answers we give aren't good enough to sustain her love of life? We told her that life is for loving and enjoying and being creative and learning. Her own suggestion was that it's for 'having fun'. I felt an almost irrepressible desire to tell her that it's for deeper things than that, but I stopped myself because

I know she already knows about some of those things; and because she will learn some of the rest soon enough. For now the serious business of having fun is so much of what it's about!

But the question did get seriously under my skin because it came at a time when I was having my own mid-life conversation with myself about what it all means. Not a crisis as such, but certainly a conversation I was taking seriously. It may be pretty hackneyed to do that at the age of 41, but for a long time now I've asked myself: 'Why would having a mid-life crisis be odd? Wouldn't *not* having one be odder? How can we accept that we are probably halfway through the time we have here and not ask ourselves what it has been about so far and what it might be about from now on? How can that not be a little scary?' Perhaps we are all having that conversation most of the time on some level or another, either more or less consciously, asking: 'What does all this mean and what does it mean to me?' But mid-life, whenever we consider that to fall these days (60 being the new 40 and all that), seems a logical time to have it, and a useful one.

So in September, as the autumn equinox approached and the light and darkness again evened out, with only a month left to go of being 40 years old, I was at a tipping point and also getting back into my portfolio-priest existence, having had a few months to adjust a little to being the mother of three rather than two children. There were lots of new things to take on, not least the increased complexity of childcare while fulfilling professional commitments, and the greater likelihood of a child being ill and needing me at a time when I was supposed to be working. I was also very aware that I had been pregnant for the last time. No longer could the prospect of procreation be a buffer against a mid-life crisis!

There were also new work challenges as the result of taking on the role of chair of governors of a secondary school. This was a vertical learning curve as my experience of how schools work these days was pretty limited, and I had never actually been a governor before. Then there was a new role as trustee of a mission agency. There I found myself among people who had much longer CVs than me and, in many cases, were graduates of universities known for their dreaming spires rather than the concrete of my own – always a tricky experience for me.

In addition to this I started to take up once more my previous commitments to BBC Radio 4's 'Thought for the Day', to being Dean of Women's Ministry and to writing this book. And I desperately wanted to do all of this without it becoming to the detriment of our family.

The autumn was, therefore, shot through with the occasional ripple of panic: panic that I'd taken on more than I could cope with; that I couldn't learn things or absorb information quickly enough; that I was out of place among the competent people around me; that I simply couldn't get through all the work I'd unwisely taken (and retaken) on. This sense of panic would ebb and flow and was almost always momentary. I'm pretty sure that no one ever noticed it, in fact I don't think it happened when other people were around. But it became an uncomfortably familiar companion. There were lots of times when I felt exhilarated and energized, moments when I loved the adrenaline rush. There were sanity-saving words of encouragement from other people, but lots of guilt about getting the balance wrong between work and home.

All of this was a reminder of our essential fragility. Perhaps I should say mine rather than ours, but I suspect not. My mother has a wooden puzzle in the shape of a tree, the sort of puzzle that is a kind of sculpture because it can stand up. It sits on the shelf above her fireplace. It is beautifully made and from the front you simply see a lovely, grainy piece of wood cut into intricate shapes that fit together perfectly. But I once picked it up and discovered that on the back it is held together with Sellotape.

It reminds me of how people mostly are. They are genuinely beautiful and on the face of it very together. The poet Andrew Motion has said about his father, '[He] was very reserved in some respects and never made a fuss about anything, but he was also a person of quivering emotionalness. He spent the last 20-odd years of his life silently weeping.'[6]

Look beyond the surface and actually most of us are held together with Sellotape in one way or another. We do need to make sure that the adhesive is of good quality and the right sort, and that we are able to admit our need for it. It may be the support of other people, of someone professional to talk to, of an activity that enables us to 'zone out' for a while (preferably a healthy rather than an illegal one). It may be the regular habit of taking ourselves out of our usual environment for sustained times of rest and reflection. All of these things have the potential to connect us with the core of ourselves that is the gift of God's mark and identity and love. We may need this particularly in times of fragility, and mid-life can produce quite a number of them.

My father would wryly use the Psalmist's phrase, 'the sickness that destroyeth in the noonday' to describe middle age. Does it feel like that? Some friends say 'No, not at all.' As general health-levels rise for those living in the developed world, many would argue that we are only beginning to reach our prime in mid-life. Some say these are the years of our lives when we will make the most impact. Mid-life is grown-up, my partner says, and grown-up involves recognizing that this is the time in our lives when we need to make a difference, if we ever want to move and shake. No pressure then! And I thought grown-up just meant buying a table runner for the first time or not looking shocked when the bill arrives in an expensive restaurant – oh, and using a briefcase instead of arriving at meetings with my dog-eared and grubby papers sticking out of my decrepit old handbag.

Mid-life is also about understanding for the first time why some octogenarians say they feel the same as they did at 21 – it's about feeling no more competent than we did then, nor confident (though I find wearing boots rather than shoes can help there, though that may not be common). It's also about an increased ability to recognize that it really is OK to make mistakes, to feel it as well as know it in your head. And it is about knowing, with Kierkegaard, that 'It's quite true what philosophy says, that life must be understood backwards. But one then forgets the other principle, that it must be lived forwards.'[7]

For me, mid-life is also about nostalgia and crying easily. Embarrassingly, I wept when listening to a class of four-year-olds singing the action song, 'My dog is a good dog', which seems rather incongruously to be based on 'My God is a good God'. Tears poured down my face as I watched the sheer, unadulterated delight with which my daughter Olivia put her heart and soul into it.

And I only have to smell, see, touch or hear something seemingly innocuous and I'm transported to a moment in my child-hood or a period of time that was formative. The experience can knock me sideways, so powerful and poignant can it be – and quite painful sometimes. I find myself identifying with the sentiments behind Sandi Thom's hit 2006 song, 'I wish I was a punk rocker (with flowers in my hair)'. What? I never wanted to be a punk rocker first time around, nor have flowers in my hair. I get confused about decades and talk about my student days as though they were ten years ago instead of twenty. I regret the passing of the past just because it's gone; and because, more pertinently, there is now less left to come.

If there is some sort of shift in mid-life with the realization that our time here is around halfway through, it seems like a good thing to reflect on and manage that shift consciously, rather than let it run away with us. One response might be to do some healthy pruning of our lives. In a profile of the TV gardener Monty Don, Kate Kellaway tells us that, 'At 53 he is starting to see how to "edit" his life. He has given up "exercising" – gardening is enough.'[8]

At 41 I'm struggling to restart exercising after a decade off, but I do like the idea of learning to edit or prune my life. Both processes bring new and better growth and avoid long-haired scraggy middle age. Perhaps we need to edit our lives well before our fifties. It probably depends on our particular circumstances and what we've accrued so far – how much of it now feels like excess, indulgence, irrelevance or just stuff that no longer fires us up or that we can pass on to others who still have the energy for it. In fact editing seems a good and healthy idea from the early stages of adulthood, in order to avoid burnout, ill health, frustration and an impossible load.

Again in the Monty Don profile, and this time with reference to his recurring bouts of depression, Kate Kellaway suggests that, 'he is like a piece of land that must have its fallow season'.[9] Fallow seasons of our life might come in all sorts of forms and for all sorts of reasons. It might be a time when our work is dull, repetitive or just not teaching us anything new; when we are recovering from an intimate relationship and for a time can be with no one else in that way; when there seems nothing new on the horizon and we're half-sad but half-relieved, because really we know we just need to lie low for a time, gently and slowly nurture ourselves or be nurtured. We do not always have to be planting and harvesting and discovering new things.

In *A Sunday at the Pool in Kigali*, Gil Courtemanche's fiction-
alized account of the Rwandan genocide, there is a character
called Valcourt who has reached middle age without really plun-
ging into life, and who fears being dead when alive.[10] There is the
fear of missing out on so much, but also the fear of losing it all
through making the 'wrong' decisions, through doing something
risky and it not paying off. There is the fear just of life being too
painful.

Life feels so precarious at times, the objects of our love so
vulnerable. Some people react by not swimming in the deepest
waters of intimate human interaction, where getting hurt is par
for the course. But surely that is a life less lived, half lived – relatively safe but sanitized.

There's a wonderful passage in Paul's Second Letter to the
Corinthians that reminds us of our fragility but also our gifts:

> But we have this treasure in clay jars, so that it may be made
> clear that this extraordinary power belongs to God and does
> not come from us. We are afflicted in every way, but not
> crushed; perplexed, but not driven to despair; persecuted, but
> not forsaken; struck down, but not destroyed; always carry-
> ing in the body the death of Jesus, so that the life of Jesus
> may also be made visible in our bodies.[11]

We are clay jars of treasure, formed of the dust of the earth,
fragile and vulnerable, easily scratched, chipped, even cracked,
carrying with us the marks of our experiences – experiences of
joy, loss, achievement, struggle, pain, insight and challenge – and
all that life has thrown at us so far, which has shaped us into
what we are.

God does not call us to be perfect works of ceramic art but to
offer all that we are, scratches, chips and all, in mending the world.
We are called to serve because we are willing to carry treasure in
clay jars, and out of the vulnerability of that way of being to
offer the treasure to others. We are called to be true to ourselves
and to grow into *being* fully ourselves, fully what God hopes and
longs for for us. For in, through and because of our fragility we
can be open to finding meaning in our experience of the world,

at whatever stage of our lives, whether the beginning, the end or right in the middle.

The woman in my godmother's clothes still looks familiar and different. She still isn't able to reach out. Meanwhile, in our shared fragility, we sit, and wait, and pray.

7

October: the bendy bus of belief
Do atheists not doubt?

London's bendy buses have been the subject of heated debate from when they were first introduced in the early 2000s. Fires on board, nostalgia for the old Routemaster double-decker buses and accidents involving pedestrians and other road users have combined to make them unpopular. Some love them but apparently many do not: they are now being phased out.

In October 2008 these buses became associated with a very different sort of controversy. The British Humanist Association, supported by Professor Richard Dawkins, launched the UK's first atheist advertising campaign. Posters appeared on bendy and other buses that declared: 'There's probably no God. Now stop worrying and enjoy your life.'

Even though it was emblazoned in huge authoritative letters across vehicles I can't avoid seeing on a daily basis, the slogan didn't exactly induce any panic in me. It did irritate me, though, because it seemed to be based on a misunderstanding of what faith is about. Faith deepens and affirms our passion for life, our joy in being human and our love of the world. How could it stop us enjoying our lives? Faith also reassures us that in times when life is tough, when our experience is shaped by sorrow and undermined by anxiety, God is as present and attentive and relevant as in the good times. So why would a believer worry any more than a non-believer or enjoy life any less?

It transpired that the campaign was a response to a very real and age-old offensive in the shape of 'wayside pulpits'. These are posters or advertising hoardings bearing grim warnings about the need to repent before it's too late. Their pictorial equivalents are those medieval paintings of the horrors of hell that show the damned receiving punishments appropriate to their specific sin. Historically many artists relished setting their fertile imaginations loose on this topic.

It's undeniable that there have also been churches, theologians and Christian leaders throughout the ages who have identified with this understanding of how God operates, and there are certainly contemporary churches that have a strong focus on the consequences of sin. Hence the wayside messages and now the atheist response.

Where religion has overemphasized our shortcomings and the terrible things that might happen to us as a result, it has given the impression that life before death has very little significance in itself. It's basically about avoiding doing the wrong thing. But this is a gross distortion of the gospel as many of us understand it. Faith can be an enticing, curious, invigorating and deeply joyful experience. It does not answer all of our questions, but it gives a framework for our lives that encourages us to explore what it means to be fully human yet made in the image of a creative, surprising, embracing and sometimes rather quirky God.

Faith in Christ can be deeply liberating, not least because it teaches us that God's love is spacious. It therefore encourages us to engage positively with those who hold different beliefs from our own. I suspect that the new brand of atheists who have become so vocal in public life in the past couple of years do not share this desire to exchange ideas amicably with those of a different persuasion. The poster campaign did say, 'There's probably no God' rather than 'There is no God', but I think I'm right in saying that this was due to advertising standards rather than the desire to preserve a spirit of open and gentle enquiry.

When researching his BBC Radio 4 series *In God We Doubt*, the journalist John Humphrys asked a lot of people the question, 'Do you believe in God?' The response was fascinating. Many of those whom he knew to be lifelong churchgoers were reticent about their beliefs and reluctant to proclaim absolutes. In the words of Humphrys himself, 'Here's the interesting thing: it was only the atheists who seemed absolutely certain.'[1] Humphrys goes on to quote his journalist friend Rod Liddle as saying:

The true scientific position, of course, is that there may be a God, or there may not be a God. Why can't we leave it at that? . . . Atheists have become terribly preoccupied with destroying God and religion and it's the absolute certitude with which they do this – and the contempt sprayed upon those who fail to share their disbelief – that worries me a little bit. History has shown us that it is not so much religion that's a problem as any system of thought that insists that one group of people are inviolably in the right, whereas the others are in the wrong and thus must somehow be punished.[2]

As somebody who might be described as a lifelong believer (so far), I do recognize the reticence of the people of faith to whom Humphrys spoke. I have great empathy with the man who begged Jesus to cure his son, and when told this would be possible only if he believed, famously replied, 'Lord, I believe; help thou mine unbelief.'[3]

There are times when I feel that belief runs through me like words through a stick of rock: right through from one end to the other, so that whichever way you cut the rock, you'll find it. I had such a moment in Westminster Abbey in the summer of 2008, listening to the choir singing about the eternal city. A sudden quick certainty about God's existence and presence, and the eternal nature of all things, took me by surprise. It was like electricity through a lightning conductor. But I also have many moments where my fumbling after belief feels more like being in a blank, blind field of mist, deeply frustrating in its refusal to yield colour, form and certainty.

Which is not why I was recently spotted on a number 18 bus, wearing rebelliously scarlet nail varnish and lipstick plus a clergy collar and reading Humphrys' *In God We Doubt*. It was less a crisis of faith and more the taking of an opportune ten minutes for research into agnosticism while on the way to a clergy social gathering (at the home of the impeccable Archdeacon I introduced in Chapter 5).

We find it hard to admit to our doubts, yet surely most of us live lives shot through with uncertainty, not in sinister or destructive ways but simply as a result of regular doses of reality and the fact that life is, actually, quite complex. Sheenagh Pugh's poem, 'What if this road', reminds us delightfully that we can never be quite sure when life might deliver another twist. The poem explores the idea that a familiar road home, known for many years, suddenly chooses to change direction and lead to somewhere else. She asks what would happen if that road decided to 'lay itself down / in a new way' and take a route via hills that hide whatever is behind them from view.[4]

We want to know what's on the other side of those hills. We want to know where the road of our life will go. So we hope and pray that we are doing the right thing in terms of choosing a partner, a job, a location, a house, a mortgage and, if we have children, a school. We weigh up the odds, we hold the options before God, we hope for a sense of 'rightness' or 'not rightness' and we take the plunge, make a decision, get on with life. We want to be 'going, at all risks'.[5]

We may be happy with where we are living and what we do much of the time. On other occasions we may question whether we made the right choices. We are not going to get all of it right all of the time and we just hope to get enough of it right for things to hang together and for us to be happy for a fair proportion of our lives.

Perhaps it is because all of this sounds so precarious that we so often see uncertainty as a bad thing. We assume that it will feel uncomfortable and disorientating. That may be true sometimes, but even when this is the case uncertainty can be a good place to be, well-positioned for going off in all sorts of directions. It encourages us to be open to life and surprises, to refuse to close down avenues of thought and therefore to leave open all sorts of suggestions, perceptions and possibilities. We live with uncertainty because nobody gave us a blueprint for our lives, and when the chips are down we probably prefer it that way.

When we were about 30 a friend and I went on holiday to Peru. It was a low-budget 'doing it authentically' Latin American experience, sufficiently adventurous for us even without the optional excursion into the Amazon, for which neither of us signed up. I returned home at the scheduled time. My friend, who is more naturally drawn to luxury hotels than Bear Grylls-style survival experiences, was lured into the jungle because of a certain male holidaymaker with whom she was willing to risk an Amazon experience.

There was a significant degree of uncertainty around this decision, as I well remember from anguished late-night conversations. But uncertainty does not have to be a sign of weakness. It can allow us the space to make uncharacteristic decisions and discover new things, even strike off in an entirely new direction. I think that my luxury-loving friend, whose wedding to the Amazon adventurer ensued, would agree.

Uncertainty can underpin our exploration of faith. It can encourage us to take risks in what we think about God rather than simply accept what we are told or have always believed. God can seem very present and then profoundly absent. In our search for meaning and the sacred, we have to be painfully honest with ourselves about our uncertainties, our fears and our demons. Otherwise what we pretend to ourselves we've discovered about God threatens to crumble to ashes and dust in our hands. That is partly why a more tentative and open approach to seeking the truth seems to open up a more interesting view.

When the architect Pugin built himself an extraordinary turreted Gothic house near Salisbury, he only put windows where he needed light or wanted a view.[6] What was he afraid of seeing? And what did he miss out on seeing by being so selective in the views he was prepared to open up? In a sense this is what we do if we refuse to allow uncertainty into our lives: decide which views we're comfortable with then carefully set our windows in positions that ensure that is exactly the view we get.

Perhaps some of us who do have a religious faith differ fundamentally from the new atheists in that we are content to live with uncertainty at least for a while and in some respects for a lifetime. And perhaps we differ also in that we are happy to engage with people who think and believe differently, to share stories and explore insights with those who live by a different framework but who are open to other people's ideas.

When my first book, *The Courage to Connect*, was reviewed in *The Observer*, the reviewer said, 'This is not a book to engage with a Dawkins or a Hitchens.'[7] Well, it was never meant to be, and neither is this, but it would be refreshing if the new atheists were to show more inclination towards engagement and less of the killer instinct. This is unlikely if they truly believe that 'religion in general is a poison that has fuelled violence and oppression throughout history, right up to the present day'.[8]

The political philosopher John Gray suggests that such a view ignores the contribution of secular despots like Stalin and Mao, and turns a blind eye to the probable connection between 'the attempt to eradicate religion and the loss of freedom'.[9] He points out that science, in which the new atheists rest their faith, has on notable occasions in the past been as wholly misappropriated as religion, citing 'the Nazi belief in race as a scientific category that opened the way to a crime without parallel in history'.[10] Gray holds that the vigorous attack on religious belief by certain atheists is not only in response to the particular terrorism that has its roots in religious fundamentalism, but to the evidence that contrary to their expectations, religion has not died as scientific knowledge has increased. As it is a bad thing, there is therefore a need to kill it. So it does not seem that the new atheists' agenda is to contribute to a debate, enter into dialogue or even to inform individuals in such a way that they can make up their minds for themselves. Rather, for whatever reason they each might have, they have set about ridiculing believers and attempting to destroy the credibility of religious faith as a viable and sane notion.

The film based on Dan Brown's book *The Da Vinci Code* is a great story about uncertainty. Those who haven't read or seen it should look away now if they don't want the surprise to be spoiled. The story is essentially that of the Holy Grail: where it might be, who might know, what it might tell us and who might be trying to suppress that information. The traditional understanding of the Grail is that it is an object, specifically, the chalice used at Jesus' Last Supper. Brown's controversial twist is the idea that the Grail is actually a line of descendants: descendants of Jesus originating from his relationship with his companion and wife, Mary Magdalene. The one surviving descendant turns out to be a petite though fortunately resourceful and robust Frenchwoman called Sophie, who is understandably surprised to discover her unproven lineage.

It remains unproven because the location of the Grail seems to be somewhere under the pyramid outside the Louvre, but only Tom Hanks works that out and he doesn't seem to intend to start digging. So even right at the end of the film we are left with a sense of profound uncertainty: is the Grail a line of descendants and is Sophie the current end of it? There is a point in the film where Hanks' character, who is a 'symbologist' caught up in Grail-mania, asks whether Jesus mightn't have been married and a father and still done all those wonderful miraculous things. It's an interesting question. Perhaps the film offers us some potentially fruitful uncertainties to muse, if only for the new thoughts they might prompt about what we believe about Jesus today.

Responding to the atheist bus campaign, Mark Vernon wrote in the *Church Times* that the evidence for the existence or non-existence of God is always open to interpretation and, with a respectful nod to Rowan Williams' writings, suggested that what really matters is the question, 'What might it be like to live a life of faith?'[11] In a Christmas meditation on faith and atheism inspired by these musings, Rupert Hoare, formerly Dean of Liverpool Cathedral, reflected that if we look outside of ourselves at two sets of people – those whose lives strike us as holy and those who need our help – we will find ourselves compelled by this 'life of genuine faith / life lived on the possibility of God's love':

> And then, if suddenly,
> For whatever reason,
> You're forced to reflect
> And look inwardly,
> Just for a moment,
> Beyond all the doubting,
> You may be surprised
> By a glimpse of the glory of love
> That is none of your making
> Yet is there in your being and doing.[12]

Perhaps there are times in our lives when, in spite of the many challenges to our faith, we catch ourselves quite simply believing, though we're not sure why or how. We read a novel or a poem that makes us see significance in small everyday things. We look at a photograph of a landscape, a flower, a child, and the sheer miracle behind the old philosophical question, 'Why is there something rather than nothing?' overwhelms us. A shaft of insight might come unbidden as we find space for our mind by strolling through a sun-drenched park or walking on a salty beach; a struggling organization or community might turn a corner.

The Scottish composer James MacMillan believes that regardless of people's formal religious commitments or conscious beliefs, music can be a way of connecting with the divine.

> Music gives us a glimpse of something beyond the horizons of materialism, or our contemporary values. What is music, after all? You can't see it, you can't touch it, you can't eat it, but its palpable presence always makes itself felt; not just in a physical way, but in ways that reach down into the crevices of the soul.[13]

There are other powerful ways to nurture the crevices of our soul so that in our own everyday experience we find ways of challenging and growing our perceptions about God. Art, poetry, friendship, holidays, work, books, family, film – all of these hold wisdom for us, particularly if we can sit for a time with uncertainty, allowing space for new understandings of God to emerge.

Andrew Motion suggests that poetry can reach the crevices of the soul because it can encourage us to be 'open to the miraculousness of the ordinary'.[14] He is honest in saying that he does not believe in God, though he goes on to say that he wishes that he did and that he can't stop thinking about it, 'so who knows what might happen one day?'[15] Perhaps the questions shape his life even if he feels he has found no answers. He reminds me of a friend at school who always said that she wanted to have faith but couldn't find it.

The 'miraculousness of the ordinary' is all around us as we meet friends for coffee, luxuriate in the Saturday newspaper, face tough issues in relationships and struggle to find effective ways of dealing with them. The crevices of our soul are reached not only by music, but art, film, theatre, literature. And of course by other people – an afternoon in the park with friends.

Nick Spencer, director of studies at the think tank Theos, has said, 'Connecting ideas with day-to-day life is something the church was once known for, but nowadays people tend not to see Christianity as a source of wisdom for living.'[16] It would be a tragedy if the Church gave up on this one. Surely it goes to the heart of what churches and preachers and believers are about, to connect the ideas of faith with our day-to-day lives; to encourage us to ask where God is in all of this.

So I say what I say, write what I write, explore what I explore, tell stories and make addresses and preach sermons and have conversations, as an invitation to people to see things from a par-ticular perspective if they find that helpful, to interpret their own lives in the light of God and Jesus if that is something that entices them, draws them out, leads them on in a direction they find creative.

The philosopher Alain de Botton has said, 'What we call "ugly" is, I think, a version of the Bad incarnate, and beauty is a version of the Good incarnate and can tug us in the right direction.'[17] It is a lovely example of the sort of common language in which those who have different frameworks but want to learn from each other might communicate.

There are plenty of people who do not believe in God but who are 'friendly to religion'[18] and those who would like to believe but find themselves unable to do so and are open to their uncertainty leading them either way. Then there are the agnostics such as John Humphrys who believe passionately that we cannot know. And then there are the believers who are quietly or even passionately reticent. Wherever we are in all of this, our uncer-tainties can lead us onwards. There may well be a God. Now stop worrying and enjoy your life.

8

November: the triumph of hope and Twitter

Myths and dreams

————◆•◆•◆————

The room was packed with year-11 pupils: for those of us who went through school some time ago, that means 15- and 16-year-olds. The occasion was the prefects' lunch, an annual event at which some of the school governors meet with the senior girls newly appointed as prefects to wish them well in their year in office.

As the new chair of governors I led a discussion session. I started fairly predictably, asking the girls to name their favourite things about the school and the things they'd most like to change. They were responsive, and obliged me with some thoughtful answers, but they were being intelligently polite rather than engaging passionately with the issues – until I threw in a final question and soon wished I'd asked it much earlier.

The date was 4 November, the eve of the American presidential election. Barack Obama's campaign had been extremely well orchestrated and funded by millions of well-wishers around the world, in touch with what was going on through the internet. Afterwards his supporters would receive a thank-you from the new President via Twitter! But at this stage the result was yet to be known and there was a barely suppressed expectation that the United States was about to elect its first ever President of black ethnic origin. The debate about whether or not it is precisely accurate to describe Obama as black had run its course. People just wanted to know now whether or not he could actually win.

So I asked the girls, 'If you could speak with Barack Obama right now, what would you ask him?' Not an earth-shatteringly clever or original question, but there was a sudden crackle of human electricity through the room and almost every hand shot up. One young woman would ask him about what sort of leader he was going to be, another wanted to know how he felt right now and another wondered what he actually wanted to achieve with his presidency. Everyone had a question.

In Tulse Hill in south London, the location of the school in question, the election of the first black President was not just about the United States. There is a very strong ethos in the school, as in many good schools where the pupils are drawn from such a wide range of ethnic groups, of celebrating all the different cultures that are represented. A high proportion of the girls are of black ethnic heritage, and the clear perception in that room that lunchtime was that the thing the United States was probably about to do, this stunning and remarkable and long-overdue history-making thing, was also about them.

In a debating competition some months later, Tosin Olukoga, a year-10 pupil, was to say: 'Obama's election hails a new era of global equality.' This is not poetic licence or a fanciful or romantic thought. A possibility that had seemed a distant dream not long ago had become fact. It was a tipping point, and nothing would be the same again.

As I write these paragraphs Obama has just achieved 100 days in office. He has already come in for some fairly sharp criticism about his handling of the US economic crisis and has made his first very public gaffe in referring to his bowling skills as being appropriate to the Special Olympics. But the fact remains that his is a fresh and inspiring voice in US and world politics, and for many the sense of excitement at what this might mean over time is still pretty close to the surface. He represents the possibility of old dreams being fulfilled and new dreams emerging.

Obama's first book, *Dreams from My Father*, is about identity and belonging. We dream dreams for ourselves, for others and for the world that is our home. Dreams bring a sense of scope and possibility. Sometimes we also know the precariousness and vulnerability of what we are hoping for. On the night that the election results were confirmed, images were beamed around the world of Obama standing in a Chicago park on what was a bitterly cold winter evening, the massive crowds greeting him with euphoric and irrepressible cheers. He looked like the most humbly triumphant man in the world – until a camera showed him to us from alongside rather than above, and revealed that he was standing behind monolithic barriers of bullet-proof glass. Suddenly he looked like the most vulnerable triumphant man as well.

Obama has said, 'Change will not come if we wait for some other person or some other time. We are the ones we've been waiting for. We are the change that we seek.'[1] To move seamlessly from world politics to the world of reality television, we will see the fifth set of contestants compete for the opportunity to work with businessman Sir Alan Sugar of Amstrad fame. We can be sure that each of them believes that they are the one we've been waiting for and that they are the change that we seek. Once again their waking dreams will be shared with Sugar-struck viewers, myself among them, who take a rather guilty delight in hearing them tell us how wonderful they are, then seeing them perform abysmally in tasks that are hardly rocket science and ending up in the boardroom dreading that phrase, 'You're fired'.

They have to be admired for their guts and tenacity, but for at least the first half of each series it is deliciously painful to watch people failing to do anything particularly constructive in order to access the dream they so desperately want to come true. There seems to be a kind of disconnect, an inability in times of panic to stop and really think about what they're trying to achieve, to get back to the basics of the task, to re-envision the outcome and to work out a process that has half a chance of achieving it. There's an awful lot of energy wasted on therapeutic (or otherwise) outpourings of angst and personal criticism, and quite often a failure to work as an effective team at the most basic level.

This changes as the number of candidates reduces, so that by the end the ones who are left are much more capable, perhaps through innate ability but also through their hard-won experience, to envisage, plan, work at and complete each task. Each of them hopes that the dream they are here to chase is gradually if indiscernibly coming into view.

There is a degree to which we can shape the future by our waking dreams and by the way we work towards making them a reality. But perhaps the future does not only come to us when we are awake. To stray for a moment onto slightly less solid territory, let's explore the potential of those dreams that we have when we're asleep. In Hanif Kureishi's novel *Something to Tell You*, the main character is a psychoanalyst. He tells us: 'I am interested in how people prepare for their dream life, for their going to bed, and how seriously they take it, lying down to make a dream.'[2]

The dreams that we dream when we sleep, over which we have no conscious control, can alarm us, delight us, disappoint us or even terrify us. Sigmund Freud told us that they can also inform us about the stuff that is floating around our unconscious and is undoubtedly forming our actions and reactions even though we are unaware of it. Those dreams are made up of bits of data that we take in without realizing it, or some of the hopes and desires that we certainly have but for all sorts of reasons suppress. Paying attention to those dreams can lead to insights we would otherwise not uncover. In a wonderful account of the place of dreams in the Bible, the distinguished American theologian Walter Brueggemann looks at the part played by our unconscious thoughts in the shaping of the world:

> We children of the Enlightenment do not regularly linger over such elusive experiences as dreams. We seek to 'enlighten' what is before us and to overcome the inscrutable and the eerie in order to make the world a better, more manageable place. We do well in our management while we are awake, and we keep the light, power and control on 24/7.
>
> Except, of course, that we must sleep. We require seasons of rest and, therefore, of vulnerability. Our control flags. We become open to stirrings that we do not initiate. Such stirrings come to us in the night unbidden. Dreams address us. They invite us beyond our initiative-taking management.[3]

Brueggemann goes on to explore four scriptural narratives about dreams that changed the course of biblical history because as a result of those dreams and their interpretation, the status quo was 'disrupted by a hidden truth designed to create new possibilities'.[4]

Jacob has just done his brother out of his birthright, and as he flees he stops to sleep, dreaming of angels ascending and descending from heaven.[5] He is assured of God's presence, protection and provision. 'When he awakes, the world is different because of this holy voice in the night.'[6]

Then there is Pharaoh's dream about seven fat cows and seven thin cows, followed by seven bulging sheaves and seven lean sheaves.[7] It is Joseph who interprets the implications regarding years of plenty and years of famine: 'Truth in the night is spoken to the one who has power in the daylight.'[8]

King Nebuchadnezzar is warned of his hubris in a dream that reduces him to a grass-eating beast. Daniel interprets it for him, and the King's power-crazed insanity is healed when he acknowledges his dependence on God.[9]

Finally Brueggemann cites the example from Matthew of the dream of the magi who, having found the Christchild, were warned not to return to Herod, who wanted to know his whereabouts in order to kill him.[10] This dream ensured, for now, the safety of God's Son in a world of vengefulness and jealousy.

We need to take our dreams seriously, whether they are the ones that emerge as we sleep or the ones that flow as we stare out of the window of the office, the kitchen or the train. Imagination should never be underestimated. Nor, similarly, the power of storytelling, which offers different perspectives and paints vibrant word-pictures of how things might possibly be if we choose to make them so. And perhaps this is where we can begin to see that myths relate to dreams and can also shape our lives, either with or without our conscious permission.

A myth, in the traditional sense of the word, is essentially an allegory. It is a story that conveys a philosophical or religious meaning. Myths were written by people trying to make sense of the world in which they lived. The events they describe may not have happened at all, or the myth may be based on history, but loosely and imaginatively. However, all myths have a meaning that the myth-tellers believed on some level to be true and that is still compelling today. 'The great old stories, the ancient myths and the sacred texts, survive and discover their value because they tell us about recurring things.'[11]

To some extent our lives here and now are shaped by contemporary myths. John Gray suggests that: 'A great deal of modern thought consists of secular myths – hollowed-out religious narratives translated into pseudo-science. [The] notion that new communications technologies will fundamentally alter the way human beings think is just such a myth.'[12]

Some of these modern stories are macro-myths, possibly designed to persuade us to a particular political point of view or to enable us to understand the economic situation. There are so-called urban myths, stories that we hear recounted about particular events or people or ideas. Our experience of a person or a place can be like a myth if the way they are described carries some of the distinctive truths about them, but misses out quite a lot of the story too. And there are myths that grow up around communities, organizations or people that tell something of the truth but may need a pinch of the salt of reality. Taken unquestioningly, myths can distort our understanding of reality. Looked at carefully, they can widen our possibilities.

The community I know best that is redolent with both myths and dreams is the church where I spent almost eight years, St Martin-in-the-Fields in Trafalgar Square. St Martin's history since 1914 has been quite literally built on a dream – and more recently on £34 million of restoration and redevelopment, which will enable the dream to continue to survive and flourish. The vision was that of Dick Sheppard, then Vicar of St Martin's, who saw:

> a great church standing in the greatest Square in the greatest City in the world . . . I saw it full of people, dropping in at all hours of the day and night. It was never dark, it was lighted all night and all day, and often tired bits of humanity swept in. And I said to them as they passed: 'Where are you going?' And they said only one thing, 'This is our home'.[13]

There is a very real sense in which this dream became a reality. St Martin's famously played host to troops heading for the trenches in the First World War, a ministry that led, at least in terms of its spirit, to the work of the Social Care Unit founded in 1948, engaged with homeless and marginalized people. The current version of that work takes place in, and has been renamed, The Connection at St Martin's, now open 24/7, still working with London's homeless people and those in danger of homelessness. The church welcomes a significant number of people who would describe themselves as vulnerable in a variety of ways, whether in relation to mental health, social unease or issues such as alcohol dependency. It is a church where people exhausted by life fall asleep in the pews and are welcome to do so.

Dick Sheppard's dream came true and still is true. But in order to ensure that it can continue, certain boundaries around people's behaviour have to be firmly implemented, otherwise chaos would reign. St Martin's can be a hard and a challenging place to be as the multifarious groups of people and individuals try to find their space there. There are the marginalized, the congregation, the café diners, the concert-attenders, the clergy, the business managers . . . the list goes on. All share the same space and all contribute to the dream, but in ways that sometimes result in what is politely known as 'creative tension'!

We live with and work with myths in our everyday lives. We need to cultivate the ability to discern the truths within them so that we do not find ourselves led astray by a misunderstanding of the story.

In his piece on biblical dreams, Walter Brueggemann finishes by looking at Martin Luther King's 'I have a dream' speech, made at the height of the Civil Rights movement in the United States in 1963. He believes that it is very significant that what King has to say is presented as a dream, because King's dream, like every dream, 'is not simply the sign of a wish or projection but is the intrusion of God into a settled world'.[14]

So back to Obama, who with his entry into the White House is considered by many to have taken Martin Luther King's dream a step further, and who like all public figures has his mythical version. Like all myths, this will be part truth, part fiction – a man who is where he is because of a powerful combination of his undoubtedly considerable gifts, the audacity of his hope, and Twitter.

It would be foolish to see Barack Obama as some sort of messianic figure, but he does seem to be a man open to the idea of dreams, aspirations and the intrusion of God. In *The Audacity of Hope* he writes of faith as an 'active, palpable agent in the world'.[15] He describes watching his elder daughter at a soccer game. She comes over to him at half-time for a drink of water, and as she runs back on to the field he says, 'For an instant, in the glow of the late afternoon, I thought I saw my older daughter as the woman she would become, as if with each step she were growing taller, her shape filling out, her long legs carrying her into a life of her own.'[16] He dreams the future.

We have to be careful with our dreams, of course, perhaps especially the waking dreams that we consciously construct and that have their own power. We have to be careful that they connect with the real world in which we forge relationships on the anvil of our own failings as well as our gifts, the world in which we face our own fragility and that of our parents and friends. Our dreams need to take account somehow of our uncertainties and our capacity to change our mind about what we think we really want out of life. The obstacles and risks involved in achieving our dreams can be trivial, quite considerable or seemingly overwhelming. And if we are fortunate enough to get there, to achieve the dream, we need to work at refusing to allow our restlessness, our thirst for perfection and our inability to live with our own weaknesses to undermine our happiness.

The power of dreams, sleeping or waking, lies in how they influence our behaviour and the thoughts and images we allow to permeate our days. The trick is to allow our imaginations to play with the possibilities; to envisage, as we would love it to be, a situation, a relationship, our idea for a new project, our hopes for a community or even a country; to imagine what might be achieved if things were done differently, what might happen if we risked making the steps that might lead to change, if we were to be audacious in our hopes and work on making them a reality.

We need to dream what we think should be done, work out what might be involved in achieving it, take the first step (generally one of the hardest things to do) and, when things get complicated and frustrating and painful, try to trust that what we are striving for is worth it. And we should always be careful that what we long for is worthwhile and creative and somehow true, and that it will in some profound sense, rather than just superficially, make us and other people happy.

Myths and dreams should be taken seriously because all of them, potentially, are ways in which God might be active in us and in the world – the God who approaches us on myriad different pathways, via our conscious and our unconscious, through stories, poetry, myths and dreams; the God who longs that we would be 'disrupted by a hidden truth designed to create new possibilities';[17] the God who waits to enter our lives through the tiniest of interstices that, when awake or asleep, we manage to leave ajar.

9

December: credit control
Chaos and a sense of direction

We spent the afternoon and evening of Advent Sunday on the motorway, returning from a trip to Lancashire to visit family and friends. It was soon dark as we travelled south, and the traffic was heavy though fast-moving.

The accidents that we saw began about two hours into our journey. There were several, one of which had clearly happened only a short time earlier. A car that had overturned was on its roof at the side of the carriageway, and as other vehicles slowed to pass safely, it seemed from the action around it that people were still trapped inside.

For me that journey had vivid resonances of Advent, with its themes of chaos, darkness and fear. With its images of wars and rumours of wars, its references to judgement and its uncertainty, Advent exudes an overriding sense that we are not in control, that it might be us next, caught up in the chaos and the drama, that ultimately no one is immune to very much.

The credit crunch has brought home some hard lessons about our ultimate lack of control over events, in this case over our financial security. The demise of Woolworths was truly the end of an era and assumed iconic significance as the crunch took a real hold on the British economy. Shortly afterwards the short-lived Zavvi reincarnation of Virgin Megastores went into administration and their shops up and down the country closed. Passing by where the one at Marble Arch had been, I saw that someone had stuck up a handwritten cardboard sign that read, 'Was definitely here once but isn't any more'.

There was something both defiant and helpless about that notice that captured at least some of the spirit of the credit crunch – 'Was definitely here once but isn't any more'. We had something and now we don't, or at least some of us don't. In fact even those of us who haven't yet lost our savings or our homes or our jobs have lost something, namely the luxury of waking up in the morning and assuming that, all things being equal, we are secure in our employment and the financial arrangements we've made for ourselves.

The realization that we are not in control of the economic situation can lead to a greater degree of honesty with ourselves about the limits of what we can control in other areas of our life. Again the atmosphere of Advent chimes forcefully with the way life sometimes seems to run away with us, and not in a good direction.

A few years ago the father of a friend suffered an unexpected illness that progressed rapidly, leading to an untimely death that left all who knew him reeling. My friend has now told me her stepmother is seriously ill. 'I cope much better when I can manage to accept that I don't have control over very much,' she wrote, but how impossibly hard it can sometimes be to reach that point of acceptance. Most of us want desperately to believe we are pretty much in control of a substantial proportion of our life, whether the big things or the mundane.

Being out of control of the mundane things can be challenging and draining. My daughter's friend emerged from school with a sticker on her sweatshirt one day bearing the statement, 'A prickly plant poked Lydia in the eye but she's all right now'. Lydia, recounting the story and her survival, looked suitably disgruntled by the unexpected and unwelcome intrusion into her day by an unfriendly organic object.

There are days when the equivalents of the prickly plant seem all too present in our lives. They introduce no major or life-changing issue, but they do build up sufficiently to irritate us severely, to make what might have been a good day into a bad day, to turn spring promise into wintry squall. We feel thwarted, our equilibrium disturbed. Our 'To do' list is only part done, or left undone, or has even been added to as a result of the prickly plant.

I admit to a quite considerable degree of control freakery. I am almost wholly incapable of sitting down to an evening's television, reading or work until all the children's toys and abandoned school uniforms are tidied away, the dishwasher is stacked and the next load of clothes is in the washing machine or transferred to the dryer. This has something to do with the need to create a relaxing, spacious and minimalist adult environment. Possibly it has even more to do with my need to control.

I need to know that I, with my partner, am in charge of the environment of our home and that even if the children do not come for their tea at the first time of asking, do not line up in a neat row to have their teeth cleaned, do not complete their homework with the commitment of embryonic university students, do not share my enthusiasm for their violin practice, do not, that is, behave as though they are extensions of my very self, nevertheless I do have control over the inanimate objects in the domestic space. And if the inanimate objects are in order I have half a chance of maximizing the order and space in my head.

Even the technologies that we purchase specifically to enable us to have greater control over our time tend to fall foul of our own ability to make sensible decisions about what we take on. I deliberately enter the phrase 'Free day' into my iPhone at regular intervals, so that looking ahead I see the most wonderful life balance emerging, with time to idle around art galleries, walk barefoot in the grass and pick more daisies. Oddly, as time goes by I very rarely reach any of those entries. Some techno-gremlin must have deleted them, replacing every one with a meeting, a talk to prepare for, a training session that will increase my competence in some new area of work. I seem not to have control over my attempt to control my diary.

And I certainly do not have control over how complete strangers respond to things that I write or say. I think this might be an appropriate moment to confess that I have been known to 'Google' myself. I started to do it because I wanted to find out where reviews of my earlier book, *The Courage to Connect*, had appeared, and where the book was being sold. It soon became a habit fraught with tension and anticipation as I failed to resist clicking on the work of various bloggers who have opinions about my opinions. It was in this way that I discovered myself on the blog site of the Vicar of Ugley, who is a real person (and Ugley is a real place), a person I've never met or encountered other than via his blog. But he has encountered me, on the radio, in the context of the 'resurrection debate' I described in Chapter 1.

On his blog is an extract from that radio interview in which I said:

> The scriptures tell us that the tomb was empty and it may well have been. Who am I to limit what God might choose to do? But my faith in the resurrection doesn't stand or fall on whether there were human remains in Christ's tomb. So perhaps it doesn't matter whether Jesus took his physical body with him. I don't think it would matter because the resurrection that I believe in, I think has continuity with what we experience in this life but in some very profound sense is about transformation, it's about something other than what we have already experienced.

Perhaps this was not very elegantly put, but it was a live interview. On the strength of it the Vicar of Ugley wrote:

> Is this anywhere close to what the Apostles preached or what the Creeds declare? Yet Rosemary Lain-Priestley is a Dean of Women's Ministry. I therefore wrote to a relevant bishop and queried how this is possible. His reply was brief, 'She's a quite articulate and intelligent liberal. But she doesn't speak for anyone apart from herself.'

The mixture of amusement, flattery and horror with which I read all this was enlightening. I resisted the temptation to email the Vicar of Ugley to demand the right to know the identity of the bishop referred to, so that I could write to him and enquire as to whether the word 'quite' was intended to qualify the 'intelligent' as well as the 'articulate' or not. For a brief time this mattered to me beyond all proportional mattering, even as I realized the vanity of the question and the likelihood of being disappointed in the answer.

But the real lesson to be learned was that once you put something of yourself out there, you can't control who sees it, what they do with it and where they send it on. We can't control how people respond to what we say, nor what they say about us as a result.

But what we can do is be sure of the overarching narrative or theme of our life and its general sense of direction. That will not – emphatically not – enable us to feel more in control, but it will help us to decide how to respond when we feel that control, always rather illusory, slipping irrevocably through our fingers. We need to know, perhaps, what our main priorities are, what are the guiding principles about our interactions with other people, what are the things that energize us and are therefore worth worrying about, and what are the issues we will refuse to let rattle us. And we need to know what are the main principles by which we live our lives, principles from which we will strive not to stray.

Since London buses found their voice, albeit an automated one, a number of strange experiences have ensued that serve as reminders of how life can take most unexpected turns. Travelling southwards towards Victoria on the number 36, we are told in slightly stilted though warm female tones, 'This is the number . . . 36 . . . to . . . Queen's Park.' This being the opposite direction to the one in which we should be going, I half-leap to my feet to be ready to get off at the next stop. Part of my brain actually believes the automated lady in spite of the evidence of my own eyes. A couple of minutes pass before I truly believe that the bus is wrong and I am right. A variation on this experience is the sudden and abrupt announcement that 'This bus is now on diversion. Please listen for further announcements' (which in practice may or may not be forthcoming any time soon).

Responses to these announcements vary. Some people leap off at the next stop, some stick around for a while in the hope that the further announcement will make things clear, others stay the full course, hoping they'll finish up somewhere close to their original destination.

It doesn't take much, sometimes, for us to question our judgement about where we are going, how and why, or to lose control of our sense of direction. Someone asks an awkward question, expects us to justify what we previously thought was obvious, looks unimpressed when we describe with passion our latest project. We stop dead in the street of our life, asking whether we should turn on our heel. Disorientation sets in. We feel out of control.

Unexpected things happen to us pretty much all the time. Some are small, some pretty big; some positive, some very hard to bear. Sometimes even the unexpected diversions that look like a very bad thing turn out to be good, and we can receive them as gifts. The Bishop of London, speaking about the economic situation, got into some trouble with the media for suggesting that an experience of redundancy can sometimes be positive because it can unleash creative opportunities and precipitate a helpful reassessment of priorities. Since the crunch began I have noticed that the letters pages of women's magazines bear some testament to the Bishop's view. But of course, as Bishop Richard would acknowledge, redundancy can also be a horrific experience, destructive, life-sapping, confidence-killing, purpose-thwarting. It can take all of our resources just to get out of bed again after being told we're no longer needed.

As we struggle with the reality that there are many things in life way beyond our control, and that the fear, unanswered questions and chaos of Advent are perhaps not just apocryphal images but relate to our own lives, the thread we might hang on to is the retention of an overall sense of direction. Then when we find ourselves unexpectedly 'on diversion' or being told we're travelling north when all the evidence suggests we're going south, we have some sense of the overarching themes of our lives and the main direction in which we're attempting to go.

In a time of economic recession one such guiding principle that our Christian faith would encourage us towards is not to neglect those with even fewer resources than ourselves. A couple of months before our Advent motorway journey, Charles Saatchi's new gallery had opened in Chelsea with a show of contemporary Chinese art. One of the exhibits was 15 naked figures made of resin, hung upside down from the ceiling by their ankles. The sculptor, Zhang Dali, explained that they represent the migrant construction workers who have quite literally built modern China, yet in economic terms are treated as the lowest of the low. Those resin human figures were shocking in their vulnerability, a vulnerability shared by the poverty-stricken in many other places.

The global financial crisis has enveloped us all with an insecurity that can cause us to overlook the situation of the most marginalized. Both for governments and for individuals, the very natural response to financial vulnerability is to look after our own, to put our energies into protecting ourselves and those immediately dependent on us. This is entirely logical and we cannot blame anyone for wanting to do it.

But whether we have responsibility for the finances of the nation, a business or simply our own household, when we narrow the horizons of our generosity there is an impact on those more vulnerable than ourselves. When governments focus sharply on protecting the incomes and assets of those who have them, those who have not can slide further into hardship. Charities that might help them are feeling the effects of the economic downturn, and businesses invest less in social enterprise projects.

Jesus said that the poor will always be with us, and so far it seems he wasn't wrong. But he also placed the vulnerable, the naked, the sick and the poverty-stricken at the very heart of his agenda, his manifesto being that all are God's children and so must be nurtured and listened to with the same loving attentiveness. People with the least social and economic capital were frequently his focus and his priority, sometimes even at the expense of his friends and family.

When our own situation is precarious it's hard to make responsible yet gracious decisions about the use of our resources. But in dire financial times there is still a moral imperative for governments, organizations and individuals to ask hard questions about what they can do on behalf of and in partnership with those who are the most economically vulnerable and therefore least able to influence their own circumstances or bail themselves out. We need to ask how we might shape a society and a world in which those Chinese migrant workers and their many, many equivalents worldwide get to share the good times as well as the bad.

On Christmas Eve we tried to go to church. The decision was to return to St Martin-in-the-Fields, where a crib service was to be led by a puppeteer. With a young family it seemed like the perfect way to spend that afternoon. But those London buses and the unpredictable traffic on Oxford Street reminded us that we can't always control how long it takes to get from A to B. We arrived too late and decided instead to visit the crib in Trafalgar Square. This new piece of public art, by the Japanese sculptor Tomoaki Suzuki, has replaced a previous crib scene that was effectively trashed during the celebrations in the square after England's rugby triumph in 2003. The old one stood open to the elements, the new one is inside a very simple glass case.

The figures are made of painted limewood and are exquisite in their beautiful simplicity. Some are modelled on people that I knew during my time at St Martin's, which always reminds me that those caught up in God's plan to radically engage with human life were themselves people like the people I know. The viewer looks at the figures from above and so gets a kind of 'God's-eye view' of the interaction between them. Joseph lies on the floor, intimately enwrapped in the miracle of his first child.

And round the other side of the crib from where I stood that Christmas Eve was our daughter Olivia, with her face pressed against the glass, looking at the scene with a kind of passive curiosity that might become a keen engagement or might dissolve into nothing as she goes off to explore something else. She spent a while there, so it seemed something was holding her attention. I wondered what she made of the story set out before her.

Advent reminds us of the lack of control we have over so many aspects of life. The prevailing economic uncertainty underlined all of that. But Christmas tells the story of a risk-taking God who embraces human vulnerability in the extreme – as a baby – in order to offer us a story, a picture, a startling revelation of how we might live out our own vulnerability in a creative way.

The Christmas story introduces us to characters who simply went with the odd and rather startling events into which they were thrown and played their part with grace, bemusement and courage as the moments continued to unfold. From them we might learn something about how to relinquish our illusions about being in control of everything, take responsibility for our responses to the challenges and gifts of daily living, and be ready to encounter that risk-taking God in a way that draws us into the story of remaking the world in love.

10

January: kissing you
Loss and connection

———◆◆◆———

Ebony Sheikh was 31 when she died just before Christmas. In the first week of January 2009 I attended her thanksgiving service, which in spite of the fact that I had never met her was one of the most deeply affecting memorials at which I have ever been present.

Ebony's mother is the headmistress of the school where I am chair of governors, and Ebony herself had been a learning mentor there. The entire school community was deeply shaken by her death. She had been diagnosed with breast cancer some two years previously, on the anniversary of the death of her father, who died aged 29.

Ebony was, from all accounts, a person so utterly full of life that it is incredibly difficult for anyone who knew her to accept that she has gone. She left a husband and six-year-old son, as well as an immediate and extended family, all of whom were shattered by her illness and death. And she had many, many friends.

Ebony was one of those people whose affirmation of others is instinctive, absorbing and time-consuming, and whose offering of hospitality was a blessing that transformed people's lives. At her thanksgiving service, people spoke of this amazing woman, of her passion for creating the perfect occasion, her complete disinterest in taking credit for any of it, her sense of humour and fun, her impeccable glamour, her refusal to give up on any of the girls with whom she worked as mentor, her sheer passion for life, her pride in her family, the exceptional love and devotion that she and her partner shared and the utter delight that she had in her son.

The thanksgiving was pretty overwhelming. One of the hardest and most poignant elements was a photographic tribute – image after image of Ebony's life with her family and friends projected on a screen. And while we watched we also listened to the voice of Des'ree, the song 'Kissing you' from the soundtrack of the 1996 film adaptation of *Romeo and Juliet*. It is a sublimely soulful piece of music in which the combination of an exquisitely beautiful piano accompaniment and stunning vocals expresses the depths of agony and ecstasy experienced in a relationship characterized by wild passion and consuming love. What made it particularly exquisite for this occasion was the fact that in the story and the song the lovers must say goodbye.

> Time can stand a thousand trials
> The strong will never fall
> But watching stars without you
> My soul cries . . .
> Touch me deep, pure and true
> Give to me for ever
> 'Cause I'm kissing you . . .
>
> Where are you now
> Where are you now
> 'Cause I'm kissing you.[1]

Ebony and her husband Ardel had been married only six years when she died. Any untimely death leaves us with a strong sense of injustice. 'It just doesn't seem fair,' we find ourselves saying, incredulously, over and over. And of course it isn't. It's grossly unjust. As a child I used to get terribly exasperated when my father told me 'Life isn't fair.' Death is even less fair, he might have added.

Ebony's thanksgiving took place on Wednesday 7 January, and on the following Saturday I was at St Martin-in-the-Fields to preach at the wedding of friends. Nick was director of music at St Martin's during my time there, and his fiancée, Caroline, was a member of the choir.

The wedding was, of course, a veritable feast of music. Handel, Parry, you name them, they were there. But it took me by surprise to find myself, during the signing of the registers, listening once again to 'Kissing you', this time performed by a pianist and vocalist who were friends of the bride and groom.

It may seem an odd choice of song for a wedding, telling as it does of the agony of parting. But it says so much about romantic love in its strongest, wildest and purest form that it was absolutely right for this occasion too.

Two events – one an ending, unbidden and devastatingly unwelcome, the other a beginning, longed for and celebrated with a passionate *joie de vivre* – with a profoundly moving piece of music held in common, a salutary reminder that when we find love we should nurture it, celebrate it, live it, rejoice in it, bask in it, swim in its depths and hold it to us right to the end. The song recognizes two profoundly life-changing human experiences, those of the deepest connection and the most traumatic loss:

> Touch me deep, pure and true,
> Give to me for ever . . .
> Where are you now?

There is a terrible inevitability written deep into the very nature of human experience, which is that the more connected you are with those around you and those whom you love, the deeper will be the wounds if and when those people are taken from you. Loss and connection are umbilically linked. To relate to someone, particularly to love them, is to open yourself to the deepest cut. This is self-evident but no more palatable or manageable for that.

During a family holiday shortly after the thanksgiving and the wedding, I watched our daughter Hannah on the tree-trekking activity. A small crowd gathered to see this small figure traversing the impossible-looking challenges of wires set like tightropes in the trees. There were spider webs, upended and suspended logs arranged in steeply ascending steps, and at one point a leap across from one platform to another that had a 20-foot drop below.

The fact is that she could not fall. She was attached to a bungee rope that in turn ran along a fixed wire between the trees. But tell that to anyone else who was completing the course. We had witnessed grown women cry on a previous visit and could see the fear in the faces of the two twenty-somethings who were following Hannah around.

If anyone fell the rope would hold them, but in frightening, swinging limbo while someone came to their rescue by a method that was not, frankly, obvious. Watching her I wondered to what extent this is our life: exhilarating zip-wires and leaps of faith, and complicated spider webs of truth; with people before and behind us on the course, some wanting to be helpful, shouting encouragement and sharing their experience with suggestions about how we might tackle the challenges; others so bound up in their own progress they barely notice us; some frozen with fear – but absolutely none of them able to live our life for us.

The hard truth is that in the end, when the chips are down, we are on our own. People can be with us through the most difficult challenges, but for so long as we are of sound mind they cannot make choices on our behalf. They can comfort and hold me but they cannot take away whatever emotional pain I feel. They can empathize but they cannot remove my bereavement. They can help me to learn about and understand myself but they cannot change me even if I want them to. They cannot learn a skill on my behalf or rise to the occasion in my place. They cannot live my friendships or be a better mother to my children on my behalf. Only I can do those things, and that is a lonely place to be. And everyone else is in it too!

It is one of the hardest things to accept about life that we are in a very real sense together with others and yet in another essentially alone. But is it not also true that all of us are held by a rope that is God's eternal and abiding love? We're not sure how and it certainly doesn't feel like it some of the time, but this is a God who is present even in our profoundest sense of absence, even in our sense of the absence of God. Christ's cry from the cross, 'My God, my God, why have you forsaken me?'[2] shows us that we are dealing with 'a God who knows the absence of God from the inside'.[3]

We are together in our solitariness and solitary in our to-getherness. These are not the thoughts of a nihilist or the product of depression or a bad day. They are simply an uncompromising description of what it means to be human.

There is a song by John Martyn that wishes for others, 'May you never lay your head down without a hand to hold'. I always want to cry when I hear it, because it is so lovely a sentiment (and because I am middle-aged and nostalgic) and because there are people who never have had anyone with whom to hold hands as they lie down, and because there are people who have had but no longer have and because some people can't conceive of how to carry on without the hand they've always held.

I hesitate to write about death in these pages because my earlier book, *The Courage to Connect*, has a chapter about mortality. To return to the subject might seem morbid or as though I have run out of themes. I am also nervous that if I mention yet again my own father's death, people will start to want to tell me to get over it. Or worse, people will expend effort in writing me a sympathetic letter or email when in fact at this stage, several years on, I need to reach inside myself to deal with the issues rather than rely on anyone else.

But what else is there in life that so surely touches each of us sooner or later? The deaths of people we care about and our own are sure and certain eventualities, and perhaps that is why the theme recurs for me and I find myself once again preoccupied with ways of thinking about it.

In a book called *The Year of Magical Thinking*, the American author Joan Didion has written about the impact of the sudden and wholly unexpected death of her husband. She says, 'Life changes fast. Life changes in the instant. You sit down to dinner and life as you know it ends.'[4] In an ordinary moment, everything changes, irrevocably and for ever.

Subsequent to her writing the book Didion's daughter died at the age of 39, and a play was written that reflected on both deaths. Reviewing the play for *The Observer*, Susannah Clapp took issue with Didion's suggestion in the book that the bereaved look different from everyone else, raw and fragile. She comments, 'Most of the bereft walk around terrifyingly unblemished.'[5]

I think she is absolutely right. It never ceases to amaze me that people survive the death of a partner, child, colleague, friend and actually pick up the thread of their lives and carry on in the face of that horrible, unremitting, incomprehensible cavern of absence:

> We buried you in the hard ground,
> Ashes in a wooden box,

The final gift of your undertaker friend.
A blanket of snow enfolded us as we stood
In silent incomprehension:
For where were you?[6]

In this fragment of a poem written for my dad, I circle around the edges of my sense of loss. It occurs to me that I have sealed up my grief for my dad in a solid wooden box like the one containing his ashes. I think I am dealing with it gradually. There is a photograph in my bedroom that for months I was unable to look at for more than a fleeting second. It was his twinkling eyes. I can meet them now for a little longer, so maybe the box is not such a bad way of handling things.

The television medical drama *Grey's Anatomy* has an episode in which two characters talk about the Dead Dad Club web site. One says that you can only be part of it once it's happened – no one can know how it feels until they've joined. 'I don't know how to exist in a world where my dad doesn't,' says the person who is recently bereaved. 'Yeah, that never really changes,' says his friend.

There are many responses to the knowledge of our own mortality. Some people simply determine to make the most of every moment. The columnist Victoria Coren believes that living every day as though it is your last is actually not possible or desirable. She argues that we need to understand ourselves in the context of a past and a future. We need to be responsible, for example, about the demise of the polar ice cap and the need to develop more social housing. And in any event, if we knew we had only 24 hours left we would be less likely to spend it fulfilling a lifetime's ambition to go scuba-diving with sharks and much more likely to curl up on the sofa with someone we love.[7]

Another response to the certainty of death is to refuse to be cowed by it. The film *A Mighty Heart* tells the story of the Wall Street journalist Daniel Pearl and his wife, Mariane, a reporter. Pearl was kidnapped in Karachi on 23 January 2002, on his way to meet with a contact. Mariane was pregnant at the time and they were due to leave Pakistan the following day for the birth of their child.

One line in this harrowing story leapt out at me, when Mariane says to her colleagues who are trying to decide how to handle the political and security issues around the search for her husband, 'We must not allow ourselves to be terrorized.'[8]

There are experiences other than bereavement that arguably affect us in similar ways, in that they are experiences of loss and remind us of the fragility of all things, and can threaten to terrorize those who are closely involved in them. In 1996 I was working in South Africa, and my partner Antony and I went on holiday to Zimbabwe, or Zim as the South Africans affectionately call it. We were there for the celebration of the sixteenth anniversary of independence. Staying in a small and friendly hotel on a bend of the Gwayi River, we wandered out into a sublime African late afternoon, the orange sun sliding towards the horizon, and came across a celebratory football match.

We were the only white people there and wondered what our reception might be, given that what was being celebrated with such joy was the end of white rule. But we need have had no fear. The welcome was of the warm and engaging African variety that offers a genuine interest in and welcome of strangers. Our sense was that these were people so fully confident in their independence and so comfortable in their own skin, nothing could rock their equanimity. Perhaps we were naive, but the experience has stayed with us through all the subsequent unrest and unspeakable heartache of that country under despotic rule. In two weeks the beauty of Zimbabwe got under our skin and into our hearts.

In London a few years later I found myself helping to host a service of prayer for the Zimbabwean people, in the presence of Morgan Tsvangirai, whose personal sacrifice on behalf of that land and its people has been phenomenal. What had happened to destroy so much? The dream of independence from white rule has turned into a nightmare because of the tyrannical reach of a dictator. So much loss and destruction for a nation to deal with. So much terror to resist.

We somehow have to manage not to be terrorized by death or other forms of loss, but this is incredibly difficult to live out. It is hard not to be paralysed by our awareness of our own fragility.

When we are dealing with these sorts of things we need all the resources we can gather, whatever they might be, in order to face down the terror and begin to live again.

My partner says that he greatly regrets that he will never see our daughters as old ladies, sitting on a park bench clutching their handbags and hopefully at peace and happy in themselves, still enjoying every moment life offers. It troubles him enormously that we can't be there for their future, even though it is the surest thing and immovable. Part of the nature of this life is the constant letting go of what is passing and changing and evolving, and in the end that will mean losing our hold on life itself. As surely as we are given the gift of living in this world we are given the certainty of an end.

A poem appeared on the London Underground as late winter approached early spring. It is called 'Brooch' and is by the Welsh-language poet Menna Elfyn. The subtitle tells us that it is in memory of Stephanie Macleod, the poet's friend. Elfyn uses the image of a brooch to perfectly encapsulate the idea that as we fashion our lives, our delicate, fragile, vulnerable, malleable lives, 'from the soft inner depth', we produce something that will be as enduring as a gemstone. The woman to whom she pays tribute fashioned such a brooch from her life and it was 'ablaze'. It will now be worn by others:

It will catch the sun. It will dazzle us.[9]

We must not be terrorized, but neither must we suppress our pain. A wise Methodist minister, Hughie Andrews, shared the wisdom of his Jamaican heritage with me when he explained the meaning of the phrase, 'Hurry-come-uppers'. Hurry-come-uppers are those who for whatever reason experience the depths of human anguish but then come back up again too quickly, not having learnt from the experience all that it might have to teach.

Making a conscious choice not to surface too quickly from experiences of loss may well be extremely painful in the medium term, but it probably makes the long term more bearable or even fruitful. James Woodward, director of the Leveson Centre for the Study of Ageing, Spirituality and Social Policy, writes:

[O]ur lives are an amazing mixture of living and dying – a continual process of movement, change, losses and gains ... The awareness of limitations and the provisionality of much of life, especially our own mortality, is an expression of living, of healthy-mindedness, as we become more integrated in ourselves.[10]

Woodward reminds us that Jesus' final meal and Passion give us the story that helps us to make sense of our lives. And it occurs to me that Jesus uses a meal to connect us both to his death and to his life, his last meal with his closest friends, celebrating the Passover, the life-giving action of God in their history, while simultaneously asking them to see the bread as his body and the wine as his blood. This in itself is a double-edged image because it points both to his violent death but also his real and substantial existence among them as a flesh-and-blood person.

And the image of a meal takes me back to Ebony and her profound gift for hospitality, for enabling people to be together. I remember that song, 'Kissing you', with its intimacy and tenderness, its passion and connection, its possessing and its loss, and am compelled by the idea that when we live well and deeply we are kissing life, with all the wonder and the risk that involves. Ebony's thanksgiving service will stay with me for a long time, because of Ebony, because of those who love her, because of 'Kissing you'.

At that service a close friend of Ebony called Maurey Lancaster, who had herself survived breast cancer, spoke with great poignancy of their friendship. She described it as an experience of falling in love. Falling in love exposes us to both the greatest pain and the possibility of exquisite joy – which is how I came to listen to 'Kissing you' twice in one week, at a funeral and at a wedding; and how I relearned the painful lesson that we live best when through all our losses and connections we take the risk of kissing life deeply.

11

February: adding laughter
God as a hands-off parent

The owner of the Lebanese café at the bottom of our street greets us warmly each time we pass by – not with words, but with a graceful action in which he indicates his heart and offers its blessings in our direction. It's a clear gesture of warm and friendly respect, and what always strikes me is that the way he does it ensures that our children are specifically included in his blessing. Maybe this is because Middle Eastern cultures typically take children seriously, honouring their presence on all occasions and genuinely engaging with them.

In Mark's Gospel people brought children to meet Jesus. Presumably they wanted them to experience something of what he was offering and to be actively included in this event, this significant moment in the life of the community. And Jesus is really annoyed with the disciples when they try to turn the children away, 'for it is to such as these that the kingdom of God belongs'.[1] In other words, heaven and earth are as much their territory as ours. For Jesus the children are very much part of the scene and are to be treated with consideration, affection and respect.

Jesus blessed the young people who were brought to him. My Lebanese neighbour does the same. But there is possibly a long way to go before we can claim that British society honours them in such a way. Some of the evidence for this lies in the tragic stories of children such as Victoria Climbié and Baby P. While it is arguable that these were relatively isolated and unfortunate incidents, there is now some data on growing up in Britain that concerns itself with more common issues that, because they are more widely experienced, are shocking in a different way.

Back in 2007 the charity Action for Children stated that: 'there is a link between the lack of resilience in children and young people and the fact that one in ten of them suffer from mental health problems.'[2] Department of Health figures showed that in a decade there had been an increase of more than one third in the number of children hospitalized because of severe eating disorders.

And in February 2009 the Children's Society published a report that was the culmination of three years' research. *A Good Childhood: Searching for Values in a Competitive Age* looked at family, friends, lifestyle, values, schooling, mental health and inequalities in relation to British children. It identified numerous unmet needs and some key issues to be addressed if Britain is to move up the league table of 'places where it is good to be a child'.[3]

All of this is in spite of the fact that we now have a generation of parents who, if they are literate or use the internet or watch television, have picked up endless tips on what constitutes good parenting and a good childhood from such sources as *Supernanny*, Mumsnet, *House of Tiny Tearaways* and Gina Ford. But the range of advice available and the divergence of opinion as to which is helpful and which is not can tend to confuse the issues rather than clarify them.

These reports about childhood serve as a salutary reminder of just how much hinges on the quality of children's relationships with their parents or, in the absence of parents, their primary care-givers. Being a parent is certainly the hardest job I have ever taken on, involving daily decisions about so many things that will form and shape our children. I find myself asking how far our relationship with them is about influencing and therefore shaping them, and how far about simply holding them and being there when they need us. How many decisions do we need to get 'right' in order to give them security and happiness?

Regarding that spectrum that has 'influencing/shaping' at one end and 'holding/being there' at the other, we read about children who are miserable because they have no boundaries and their parents are very hands-off, and about those who are constrained by parents who are too controlling. What do we need to take seriously in order to get somewhere close to achieving balance?

And can the idea that we are God's children and that God in a sense is our parent inform these questions at all?

It probably sounds like a very simplistic statement to make, but in seeking the balance between influencing and simply holding our children, we have to take relationships seriously. Even between mature adults, relationships are incredibly complex, nuanced and potentially fragile, while paradoxically pretty robust in that broken relationships can be mended if the people on both sides want that to happen. Even when there is parity between the parties, relationships between adults can be hard to negotiate. We can so easily get other people wrong, even those we know intimately. Colleagues can either be potential best friends or a complete mystery to us. Even our friends vary from those with whom we are completely at ease and those whom we quite simply never fully fathom, however long we know them. And as for families . . .

So it should be no surprise that relationships between parents and children and between ourselves and God as our Creator-parent can be quite complex.

Joseph Isaac Lain finds a lot of things very funny. His deep chuckles are incredibly infectious, so his sisters do all that they can to make him laugh, often inducing an uncontrollable fit of giggles that has us all joining in. We have always chosen our children's names for their meaning as well as their sound. Joseph means 'the Lord added to the family' and Isaac, appropriately as it turns out, means 'laughter'.

In Genesis 18 we find the beginning of the story of another Isaac. Sarah overhears messengers from God telling her husband Abraham that they will have a son. She laughs, not out of sheer delight but because she is way past childbearing age and simply does not believe it's possible.

I love the fact that Sarah dared to laugh at God's intentions. She was amused by the ambitious reach of God's plan for her, not thinking for a moment that it would be fulfilled. It was the laughter of a woman of spirit who had shaped her whole life around a desire that had never been fulfilled and who at this late stage could still laugh about it; of someone who was shortly to discover that her longing was to be met after all, exactly when she least expected it and was probably least prepared. She would need to hold on to that sense of humour.

But the story goes on of course with God's challenge, 'Is anything too wonderful for the LORD?'[4] So the child is born and because of Sarah's laughter is named Isaac.

And as I read this story and ponder this name, it strikes me that in all the potential and fragility, glory and tension of human relationships, laughter is an enormously helpful thing! It is the most fantastic tool within relationships because if we can laugh together we can probably relax together, and it's when we relax that we allow one another more space to be what we are. Things that might otherwise not be explored can begin to emerge in this safe space. Humour, if it is a mutual and loving thing and carries no hint of anybody being laughed at, can enable profound grace and generosity within relationships.

Of course this sounds very simplistic, and when we are in the middle of a stand-up row or reaching a flashpoint with our partner or children, our siblings, parents or friends, the last thing that we want to do is laugh. So I don't mean that laughter is a simplistic fix-all to be taken up at random and at the risk of escalating the row by irritating the other participant. Rather I wonder whether the amount of laughter we can encourage in a relationship while it is on an even keel might have a bearing on how we manage the difficult phases together. And I do think there can come a moment even in the middle of a horrible altercation when something unintentionally funny is said and there is an opportunity to allow laughter to surface, bringing with it its healing power.

At the National Theatre last year I saw Lucinda Coxon's play, *Happy Now?*. With excruciating accuracy of tone it traces the disintegration of the lives of a group of pseudo-friends, couples who might be described as pretty privileged and high achieving. Kitty is a working mother who currently does almost everything that needs doing at home and is at the same time taking on increasing responsibilities in her work for a cancer research charity. She hasn't stopped in a long time to ask herself whether or not she's happy, so when a very unlikely man hits on her at a conference she is shocked by how 'unsteady' she feels as a result.

Bea meanwhile is trying to achieve the perfect life through designing the perfect home. She always needs a project or she starts to fall apart. Her husband Miles is bored and cruel to her, and there's a huge amount of anger simmering between them. He is very bitter about being married to somebody whom he describes as an 'endlessly hungry permanently empty thing'.

Kitty's husband Johnny has given up a well-paid job to do something 'useful' as a teacher in a state school and to regain some work–life balance, but is overworked and exhausted. He commits the cardinal sin by telling Bea that her daughter Hettie, who is apparently gifted ('Officially gifted,' Bea declares, 'They tested her'), is not in fact gifted at all.

Quietly in the background Kitty's friend Carl, assumed to be blissfully happy with his new boyfriend, deals with the breakdown of that relationship without mentioning it. And Kitty struggles with her unanswered questions about the rift between her parents.

The play concludes with each character, palpably bruised, attempting to regain some sort of stability within this heap of mangled egos, identities and relationships. One of the many striking things about this powerful piece of theatre is how little laughter there is in the characters' lives, other than that which is cynical, weary or desperate. Plenty of laughter from the audience, though that too has an edge as people recognize in these scenarios more than they are comfortable to acknowledge as familiar. But there is very little amusement on stage.

Perhaps the amount of laughter in a relationship is some sort of barometer of its health. It can certainly be an instrument of healing.

So what part does laughter play in our nurture of children? Our seven-year-old told us the other day that children laugh 400 times a day and adults laugh just four times. I'm not convinced she has the figures right, but I think we get the message. We may think we laugh a lot but we could do more! One of the most important things we can do for our children is to encourage rather than silence their laughter. Encouraging that laughter deepens and enhances our relationship with them, and encourages in them a significant gift that they can then offer in all of their relationships through their growing up and into adulthood. When they are consumed by gales of laughter at something we consider to be silly or inappropriate, it is easy to demand unthinkingly that they pay attention to something more serious. At other times we are just so busy that we fail to respond when they ask us to share in what they find so delightful or funny.

And yet on other occasions they simply have no idea how funny they are. Over the winter of 2008 to 2009 our daughters became obsessed with the film version of *Mamma Mia*, watching the DVD so many times they could rehearse whole conversations from it and sing and perform all the songs inside out. For the uninitiated, the story is woven around the songs of Abba, though the significance of Abba is of course lost on them.

The film is about a girl called Sophie who is about to get married. She wants to invite her father to the wedding but therein lies a problem. She was born nine months after a particularly busy summer in her mother's life, and there are three possible candidates for the role of dad. The precise logistics of this issue are beyond our daughters' understanding, but they do get the fact that Sophie doesn't know whether her father is Harry, Bill or Sam.

I had not laughed so much in a very long time as on the morning when a friend felt bound to tip me off that my daughter Olivia, who has a tendency to empathy and drama, had been telling her friends at school that she doesn't know who her father is, but that she does know that he is either called Harry or Bill or Sam. Not having seen the film my friend was mildly curious, and felt it only fair to warn me of the reason for the scandalized glances I might be about to get in the playground, perhaps particularly from those aware I'm a priest. It's fortunate Olivia is the spitting image of her father.

Children add laughter to our lives, among so many other things. Part of me wonders wryly whether God feels the same about us. Turning to the question of ourselves as God's children and God as parent, what might we learn about the relative merits of hands-off or hands-on parenting? If it doesn't seem too odd a thing to say, it strikes me that in some ways God is a pretty hands-off parent, at least by our current standards. And that is by no means a wholly reassuring thought. Long silences from a parent whose affirmation, support or advice we crave are not generally the most helpful thing. We can spend quite a lot of our lives wondering where God is when we need something specific from our originator and supposed friend. We might need clear guidance on an issue that we have looked at from every angle and simply cannot resolve. We might need holding in our fears or distress or anxiety. We might want to know what is the next step for us in our life's development and value some pointers as we consider different options. We might feel the need to be reassured that we have security in God even though our financial security is highly precarious.

A God who gives us lots of space is not necessarily easy to live with – or without. Michelangelo's fresco, *The Creation of Adam*, says something into this dilemma, a pictorial expression of this issue about a hands-off God. Adam is lying back, his outstretched hand reaching almost languidly in God's direction. God is stretching forward towards him. Their index fingers are almost touching, but not quite. God is about to breathe life into Adam. They are not embracing or even facing each other square on. There is a spaciousness about the picture that does seem to echo our own experience, much of the time, of a God who certainly does not impinge on our day-to-day decisions and activities, and who in fact can feel quite remote.

So God as a hands-off parent can present us with serious challenges, but perhaps if we can live with the prevailing sense of absence at times, the relationship on offer can also be quite grown-up in a good way. God seems to offer a kind of easy, spacious intimacy that allows us to explore ourselves and our lives with impunity, while always knowing where our home is. God gives us resources and tools with which to negotiate our way from childhood to maturity: the richness of scripture, the lives of other people, the lessons that we learn from the created world, the still small voice within ourselves and, for some, the wisdom and guidance of good human parents.

The fact that our Creator retains a pretty light touch means I can ignore God for a very long time without any fear of being thrown out of the parental home. I can rail and shout and lay the blame at God's feet for all sorts of things, and I know that our relationship will not be damaged. What does that say to us about God? Presumably it's that the divine forbearance, patience, courage, stamina, fortitude, irritation threshold, capacity to forgive, ability to cope with rejection and sulking, are far better developed than mine will ever be.

To balance our perception that God has a light touch we per-haps need to remind ourselves of the Jewish and Christian scrip-tures with their plethora of stories gathered and recorded down the ages in communities seeking to work out their relationship with the Creator they believed to be the source of their being. Those stories do speak of the transcendence and remoteness of God but also of the tremendous intimacy between human beings and their Creator, who is concerned with the whole of a person and his or her day-to-day life.

If it sounds as though I'm contradicting everything I've just said about God's remoteness, that is because no discussion of God gets far without some sort of paradox emerging. God can be intimate and God can seem terribly absent, and we cannot control when and how the balance plays out. We can only ride with it, perhaps rejoicing in the advantages of both 'parenting approaches'.

There is a brief poem by the Sufi Master, Hafiz, called 'Laughing at the word two'. It celebrates the paradoxes of God's relationship with us and speaks of God's laughter:

Only
That Illumined
One
Who keeps
Seducing the formless into form
Had the charm to win my
Heart.
Only a Perfect One
Who is always
Laughing at the word
Two
Can make you know
Of
Love.[5]

The delicate blend of formality and intimacy in this poem cap-tures some of what we might feel about how God relates to us: the distant 'illumined' one who laughs at the thought of having a companion; seduction and charm alongside perfection. There is a sense of relaxed intimacy, formlessness and form, laughter and love that is almost intoxicating, a relationship that offers just the right balance of space and connection.

I long for many things in my faltering and frequently not quite good enough parenting. I long to achieve the right balance between managing my children's behaviour and yet allowing them the freedom they so clearly relish and I as an adult would give my eye teeth to recapture – that freedom of thought that allows them to ask any question, no matter how odd it sounds to a grown-up, in the expectation of being taken fully seriously and given a satisfactory answer; that freedom of body that is expressed as they throw themselves crazily around the living room practising their gymnastics, or run through the park with faces to the sky on a breezy spring day; that freedom of imagination that takes them on night flights on their magic ponies, exploring new places and revisiting old with no spatial limitation.

As I write this I wonder whether much of that is what our Creator wants for us. God creates, breathes life into creation, steps back into the shadows but is always there, watching and in some sense holding us, longing for us to be all that we can be, willing us freedom and wishing us playfulness, rejoicing in our laughter and silently encouraging the growth of our relationships.

While talking with a friend about the 'Shall we try for a third one?' dilemma, she said that looking at her two daughters made her ponder with barely containable glee, 'I wonder what we can make next?' I find myself curious whether God has that same sense of excitement at the sheer miracle of bringing something out of nothing – of bringing everything out of nothing, adding beauty, adding pain, adding joy, adding laughter, and each time in the knowledge of the breathtaking potential that every new person brings to the world.

12

March again: the sublime in the ridiculous
Making holy ground

———◆———

So as this year of consciously downloading my life begins to draw to a close, and as we approach another spring equinox, what is happening? Well, the credit crunch has not gone away, politicians are still being lambasted for getting their responses to it wrong, and the sense of no one being in control is still with us.

By the end of the month media personality Jade Goody will have died a very public death, and in her dying have transformed the way a lot of people perceive her. She has encouraged many young women to take more responsibility for their health and has set about affirming the most important relationships in her life, while making connections between the here and now and what might come after. She seems to have done all of this with imagination and courage.

As I queue in the bank, on a television screen above the counter I can see the Conservative Party leader David Cameron setting out a proposal for reforming financial regulation. It is only a couple of weeks since the tragic death of his son, Ivan. Cameron looks as he always looks, youthful and a little overscrubbed, and I remember the journalist Susannah Clapp's claim (Chapter 10) that the terrifying thing about the bereaved is that they look just like the rest of us.

From Northern Ireland we are hearing the news of the first deaths of British soldiers in 12 years. I remember that on the Craigavon Bridge that joins Londonderry's mainly Catholic and mainly Protestant areas, there is a bronze sculpture of two male figures each extending a hand towards the other across a divide.

The gap between them pretty much equals the length of their arms at full stretch, and there's an effort involved in not losing their balance. Right here, right now, the people of Northern Ireland are showing their determination not to lose that balance. The voices of people in both communities have already risen in protest at the shootings.

Watching the film *Slumdog Millionaire*, I marvel at the tenacity of human nature, at the ability of some people to survive being born into the most dreadful and unpromising circumstances and to carve out lives that have beauty, truth and meaning. And I notice that the central character in the film manages to answer every question in the quiz show simply because each answer has a connection with a particular event or phase in his life. He is downloading his experiences, making connections, sometimes recognizing for the first time the significance of things that he has known only subconsciously.

I live in a second-floor flat in a street of apartment blocks. I don't deliberately spy on people but it's hard not to notice some things about the lives of those who live on the other side of the street. The neighbours opposite pray a lot. I know they do because I watch them. At odd times of the night I glance out of the window, and because their lights are on and their curtains open, I can't help but see them, prostrate in a corner of their dining room, enrapt in prayer. There's a simple and beautiful rhythm to their actions: their rocking forward on their knees and their sitting back on their heels.

Then when they've finished they take up their mats and carry on with daily life, go back to the conversations they were having with their wives and daughters in the living room, carrying with them that golden thread of attentiveness to God that is woven through their lives. The presence and commitment of these Muslim men, and their rhythm of praying and living, praying and living, praying and living, has become part of the backdrop to my own life, and I'm so grateful for it. It reminds and reassures me that there is a God to be attended to and that some people are doing some attending while I go about my own daily life and even while I sleep.

We're on waving terms with the family that pray, which matters to me because both the praying and the waving connect us.

The street is more holy because of their smiles and because of that corner of their dining room, made sacred by their prayers. My life is more holy because as I see them pray, so often and so faithfully, so privately and so deliberately, I'm reminded of God's presence in the dining room of daily life and in the living space of human activity.

The Palestinian poet Mahmoud Darwish, who died in August 2008, left a last poem, 'The dice player'. Poetry is so many-layered and allusive that it can mean very different things to those who read it, but I think that what Darwish is saying in this poem is that all sorts of things happen that result in us being alive in a particular time and place, and that his response is to live life where he is rather than look for life elsewhere. He tells us:

> only by chance did the land become holy:
> . . . a prophet set foot there
> and when he prayed on a rock it wept . . .[1]

We make holy ground of the places where we eat, sleep, walk, play, weep and love. We make holy ground of the relationships we inhabit. We make holy ground of ourselves. But the holy, the sacred, is there in embryo already. We both make the ground holy and discover that it already is. We make it real, to ourselves and others, by noticing it.

Perhaps this is what Moses experiences at the burning bush, or non-burning bush as perhaps it ought to be known. In Exodus 3 we read:

Moses was keeping the flock of his father-in-law Jethro, the priest of Midian; he led his flock beyond the wilderness, and came to Horeb, the mountain of God. There the angel of the LORD appeared to him in a flame of fire out of a bush; he looked, and the bush was blazing, yet it was not consumed. Then Moses said, 'I must turn aside and look at this great sight, and see why the bush is not burned up.' When the LORD saw that he had turned aside to see, God called to him out of the bush, 'Moses, Moses!' And he said, 'Here I am.' Then he said, 'Come no closer! Remove the sandals from your feet, for the place on which you are standing is holy ground.' He said further, 'I am the God of your father, the God of Abraham, the God of Isaac, and the God of Jacob.' And Moses hid his face, for he was afraid to look at God.[2]

This is Moses' moment of revelation, his sudden perception that the ground is holy and that he is required to pay attention to it. If we pay attention to our experience it is sacred and can speak to us of God. But some experiences are more sacred than others because we make them so. We listen with particular keenness, wait with a particular expectation, look with a particular attention that requires every muscle of our spiritual sensitivity – our antennae, our radar, our ability to sense God's presence.

So to make meaningful connections between God, ourselves, the world and others, we need to be serious about trying. We need to do the job of a prophet, falling on the rocks and praying in order to make them holy ground.

With Moses we're called on our journey to turn aside and see, not to be afraid to discover God. We're called to make the land holy for ourselves and for others. All of this is prayer: the turning aside, the seeing, the not being afraid – and the being afraid too, and the making holy. This prayer will take many, many different forms, but it will always be about life's ordinary magic – the sacredness of human relationships, of ideas, of green fields in driving rain, of coffee shared with a friend as we spill our soul before her.

How urgent is it that we do this? Well, perhaps we could equally well ask how urgent it is that we don't squander our lives. One survivor of the Spanish air crash in the summer of 2008, interviewed by a journalist, said 'For us it is a day to celebrate our lives.' Such stories offer us a momentary shock at our good fortune to be alive. We still fail to pay much attention to the sacred quite a lot of the time, but the wonder of it is that for so long as our lives here continue, God's love is renewed every morning, and each day brings opportunities to pay attention, to unwrap the sacred, to discover the divine, to connect with God in the reality of life.

Over 40 years the attempt to connect has become something of a habit for me, and I feel compelled to ask where God is even on the days when I know before I ask the question that the answer will come in the form of a resounding silence.

I love that story about Elijah in the desert, listening for God. And God is not in the wind, or the cloud, but in the still small voice that he barely hears. We know all about that. Even then we think it's our own voice, and it may well be sometimes, but we cultivate the habit of listening for the sake of those moments when the connection comes: when our own life, the lives of others, the life of the world and the life of God seem to have something in common.

That something is wonderfully inextricable, a something that offers hope and the opportunity to grow, to begin to move on from where we were a moment ago, to become someone and something who, because we have connected with the holy ground on which we walk, has discovered and unwrapped the sacred.

The Gospels describe Jesus as a man of many windows and lenses, who somehow set aside religious and cultural prejudices in each encounter with a new person. Even his previous experience did not seem to cloud his judgement. He had a way of connecting with the entirety of somebody so that their illness, their question or their particular struggle was just part of what he saw. Hence he noticed people who were used not to being noticed, such as blind Bartimaeus,[3] and he was interested in the whole of somebody's story, like the Samaritan woman at the well,[4] whose personal history he unfolded much to her surprise. He took a broader and deeper view than we often do.

In the living of our lives it is so easy to let the ordinary slip through our hands like sand, not realizing that every particle of life is like gold-dust, to be wondered at and gloried in; and that for a time we hold a miracle in our hands, the miracle of simply being rather than not being.

The most popular Gospel reading for weddings is the story of Jesus at the wedding in Cana of Galilee, where he turned water into wine. There are obvious connections and there are deeper ones too: 'When the wine gave out, the mother of Jesus said to him, "They have no wine" . . . [and] said to the servants, "Do whatever he tells you" . . . Jesus said to them, "Fill the jars with water."'[5] Water in this Gospel story represents the ordinary, the day-to-day, the mundane, which is nevertheless vital for life to be lived at all; the water that has within it the potential to be changed and to become the wine of joy and of celebration, reminding us of the depth and colour of life, enticing us to taste and savour and relish all that it can offer.

The fact that it is water that becomes wine reminds us that what is most valuable and real and true in our lives, what can most bless us, is often found in the seemingly ordinary, which turns out not to be ordinary at all. And the fact that it happens at a wedding tips us off to that glorious truth: that until we explore them we will never know which relationships are going to lead us into a greater sense of fulfilment, otherness, connection, intimacy and sacredness; which will begin as water and mature as wine. This applies to friendships and to relationships with colleagues. It may even have something to say to how we relate to family. And it is certainly true of the partnerships we explore in the hope of finding someone with whom to share our lives on the deepest level.

The wedding guests did not know that the water was wine until they drank it. Relationships cannot be explored in theory, and however vulnerable it might make us feel, they require from us an openness and willingness to take risks. There are many un-answerable questions at the beginning of intimacy. There is the obvious 'Will we make this work?' 'Dare I take the risk?', and the more complex 'Is this the sort of quirky-looking match that is the stuff of fairy-tale endings or the sort of quirky-looking match that is a disaster-in-waiting?'

We discover the extraordinary by paying attention to what is before us and seeing where it might lead. Here are some things that are not ordinary.

A hotel kitchen in Zimbabwe: we come down to the dining room for our Sunday breakfast and can hear beautiful, resonant, African voices singing in harmony. Through a door to the kitchen set a little ajar we glimpse the cook, smiling broadly, conducting her kitchen staff with a ladle. The song finishes, the group disperses. God has been worshipped and breakfast is served.

And something else: Douglas Board, chair of the Friends of The Connection at St Martin-in-the-Fields, a central London homelessness charity, tells of a night spent with one of the charity's workers out on the streets of central London:

I doubt I have ever seen more Christ-like work than Adrian's, moving from doorway to doorway, calling people by name, turning away when not wanted. As is ever God's way, it is work done through believers and non-believers, through Jews and Gentiles, saints and sinners. And without knowing it, Adrian changed my picture of Jesus. I don't suppose Jesus smoked roll-ups, but that night I saw something eerily similar between Adrian and his roll-ups and Jesus and his parables. I can imagine walking for two hours with Jesus up and round Covent Garden, Embankment and Charing Cross, while the night life swirls around us. Suddenly he stops on a street corner, gets out his tin of experience, straightens out his words, moistens his lips, lights a flame and says – 'Listen! A sower went out to sow.'[6]

And something else: 'I hope you're going to write about the sacredness of having coffee with friends,' said a friend, over coffee. Why is drinking coffee with friends so important? It is because when I talk I can breathe again, I can download things I've been carrying and so can the person with me. We can discover common experiences and marvel at our differences too. It's my therapy, just wittering with friends. That's what is sacred about coffee.

We are talking about different ways of knowing God. In the Hebrew and Christian scriptures, 'knowing' is always about entering into, and so it's about entering into God everywhere, taking the stuff of our everyday lives and through it entering what is within it. Anne Dyer, Warden of Cranmer Hall Theological College in Durham, says it is essentially a 'habit of relating'.[7]

Speaking about his secondary school English teacher, the poet Andrew Motion said, 'He walked into my head and turned the lights on, and made connections that I've never really broken ever since.'[8] Motion himself wrote a poem that is essentially about connections, and which is etched around the handrail of the lightwell that brings daylight into the new underground spaces of St Martin-in-the-Fields. A spiral staircase leads down into the crypt, but from the lightwell there is an amazing view of the outside of the church, the spire reaching up gloriously to the sky:

> Your stepping inwards from the air to earth
> Winds round itself to meet the open sky

So vanishing becomes a second birth.
Fare well. Return. Fare well. Return again.
Here home and elsewhere share one mystery.
Here love and conscience sing the same refrain.
Here time leaps up. And strikes eternity.[9]

Time and eternity are intertwined. Our dreams are edged with reality. We need to draw on eternity to feed temporal time and we can because they are umbilically connected. In our living we unearth, unfold, unwrap and see the life within our life. This habit of uncovering the holy can become a framework for our lives, offering new perspectives and relationships between events, people and God every day.

The philosopher Alain de Botton has said:

I get distressed at the thought of ideas not finding a home in day-to-day life, and similarly of day-to-day life going by without the interpretation I think it can sustain. People will say, 'Oh, this is just an ordinary moment' or 'just an ordinary event' and I'll always think: Yes, but you can compare it, contrast it and connect it to something else.[10]

Everything comes to have significance in relation to something else as we build a web of intricate pathways in our lives, in our relationships and even quite literally in our brain. And, I would argue, as that happens we can begin to make some sense of God. We discover God in the connections and the ideas, the patterns and the web of awe and wonder that is ever-growing as our lives progress.

We need to live the so-called ordinary stuff of our lives in such a way that when we look back there are as few moments as possible when we failed to pay real attention, to share our thoughts freely with one another, to wonder at the sheer wonder of it all, because if we prepare well for our dreams and live them with courage, imagination and understanding, water can become wine.

So in this new time and place that happens to be March 2009, because I want to uncover the sacred in life, because I am compelled to look for meaning, I'm seeking ways to make holy the ground on which I walk and the journey on which I'm led. We are all called to do that as the phases of our lives progress and we meet new people, discover new things, explore new places and learn to be together in different ways. We gather insights through relationships and community, music and art, global crises and national events, work and playfulness, silence and words. We discover the divine in the detail and probably the sublime in the ridiculous.

And we will never cease to be surprised by the sacred as we celebrate it, stand in awe of it and often give thanks for it. It can be utterly breathtaking, or we may find it in the things we had considered to be most mundane until we noticed them properly for the first time. But in whatever form it comes, the sacred can transform us as we gradually unwrap it in the people, events, moments and places of our gloriously unfolding lives.

Conclusion

There is a rather wonderful harvest hymn that celebrates the miracle of creation and finishes with the words:

> For the wonders that astound us,
> for the truths that still confound us,
> most of all that love has found us,
> thanks be to God.[1]

We live out of the conviction that amid the astounding wonders and perplexing truths that make up our lives, love has in fact found us, recreated us and placed us where we are meant to be with those we are given to care for, and that in loving one another we are to reflect God's love in every aspect of our lives.

We are called to live those lives with optimism and wonder, with enchantment, with holiness and with passion, and in the sure and certain knowledge of the underpinning, overarching and all-sustaining love that has sought us out and found us as surely as we have been born.

I set out to sift through the happenings in a year of my life and the life of the world, and to do it consciously and deliberately. I expected some of what I encountered in that year to be familiar and some things to be new and different, possibly even difficult. I wasn't wrong! There were fresh experiences and familiar ones, new relationships and those that have been around for a long time. There were considerable learning curves and many familiar tasks. There was a changing world stage with many of the same characters and scenery on it, but some exciting new players.

For all of us each year will be the same but different. Each will bring challenges, hopes, fears and possibilities, but in all of this and in all of our lives there is the potential to unwrap the sacred in everything around us, to find the sublime and the glorious deep within ourselves, and to discover the divine in the unfolding year.

> For the wonders that astound us,
> for the truths that still confound us,
> most of all that love has found us,
> thanks be to God.

Notes

1 From March into April: equinox moments

1 From the Chrism Eucharist, 'Passiontide and Holy Week', *Common Worship: Times and Seasons*, London: Church House Publishing, 2006, p. 285.
2 Suzanne Goldenberg, 'Bush's last plea', *The Guardian*, 29 January 2008.
3 Mrs C. F. Alexander, 'There is a green hill far away', *The English Hymnal*, London: SCM-Canterbury Press, 1986; new edition.
4 Andrew Motion interviewed by Andrew Rumsey, *Third Way*, vol. 32, no. 3, April 2009, p. 20.
5 From the Exsultet, 'The Easter Liturgy', *Common Worship: Times and Seasons*, London: Church House Publishing, 2006, p. 337. Permission sought from The Archbishops' Council.
6 Revelation 21.1.

2 May: the back ends of buildings

1 Babylonian Talmud, Ta'anit 9a.
2 Micah 6.8.
3 Rabbi Mark Winer, '*Tikkun Olam*: A Jewish theology of "repairing the world"', *Theology*, November/December 2008, p. 440.
4 Winer, *Tikkun Olam*, p. 434.
5 Douglas Board, 'Seeing and not seeing', sermon for Homelessness Sunday, St Martin-in-the-Fields, 1 February 2009. My thanks to Douglas for providing me with a copy of his sermon and his permission to quote from it.
6 Mark 6.5.
7 Matthew 3.2; my paraphrase.
8 Winer, *Tikkun Olam*, p. 440.

3 June: for the sake of friendship

1 Mark Vernon, *The Philosophy of Friendship*, Basingstoke: Palgrave Macmillan, 2005, p. 135.
2 Vernon, *Philosophy of Friendship*, p. 58.
3 Trevor Dennis, *The Easter Stories*, London: SPCK, 2008, p. 13.
4 Dennis, *Easter Stories*, pp. 13–14.
5 Dennis, *Easter Stories*, p. 15.
6 Dennis, *Easter Stories*, pp. 13–14.
7 Doris Lessing, *The Grass is Singing*, London: Michael Joseph, 1950.

4 July: bringing it all to the party

1 *The Sunday Telegraph*, 14 April 2008.
2 Kira Cochrane, 'You're fired', *The Guardian*, 23 April 2008.
3 Lola Young, 'Brilliant baronesses', *The Guardian*, 7 May 2008.
4 Hillary Clinton, Concession speech, Washington DC, 7 June 2008.
5 Review of Rachel Cusk's *A Life's Work: On Becoming a Mother* (London: Fourth Estate, 2001), quoted by Rachel Cusk in 'I was only telling the truth', *The Guardian*, 21 March 2008.
6 As reported in *Mail* Online, 28 March 2007.
7 Susan Durber, *Preaching Like a Woman*, London: SPCK, 2007.
8 Barack Obama, *The Audacity of Hope: Thoughts on Reclaiming the American Dream*, New York: Crown, 2006, pp. 207–8.

5 August: the Maria von Trapp of Marylebone

1 Hanif Kureishi, *Something to Tell You*, London: Faber & Faber, 2008, p. 4.

6 September: the woman in my godmother's clothes

1 Luke 19.1–10.
2 Luke 18.18–25.
3 Luke 10.38–42.
4 John 11.27.
5 Oliver James, *Affluenza*, London: Vermilion, p. xvi.
6 Andrew Motion interviewed by Andrew Rumsey, *Third Way*, vol. 32, no. 3, April 2009, p. 19.
7 Peter P. Rohde (ed.), Søren Kierkegaard, *The Diary of Søren Kierkegaard*, trans. Girda M. Anderson, London: Peter Owen, 1961, p. 111.
8 Monty Don interviewed by Kate Kellaway, *The Observer*, 8 March 2009.
9 Don interviewed by Kellaway.
10 Gil Courtemanche, *A Sunday at the Pool in Kigali* (trans. Patricia Claxton), Edinburgh: Canongate, 2003.
11 2 Corinthians 4.7–10.

7 October: the bendy bus of belief

1 John Humphrys, *In God We Doubt*, London: Hodder & Stoughton, 2007, p. 328.
2 Rod Liddle, quoted in Humphrys, *In God We Doubt*, p. 330.
3 Mark 9.24, Authorized Version.
4 Sheenagh Pugh, 'What if this road', in Neil Astley (ed.), *Being Alive*, Tarset: Bloodaxe Books, 2004, p. 37. Reproduced by permission.
5 Pugh, 'What if this road'.

6 'God's architect: Pugin and the building of romantic Britain', *Book of the Week*, BBC Radio 4, 12–16 November 2007; abridgement of Rosemary Hill, *God's Architect: Pugin and the Building of Romantic Britain*, London: Allen Lane, 2007.

7 James Purdon, *The Observer*, 16 December 2007.

8 John Gray, 'The atheist delusion', *The Guardian*, 15 March 2008.

9 Gray, 'atheist delusion'.

10 Gray, 'atheist delusion'.

11 Mark Vernon, 'What really matters is the life of faith', *Church Times*, 31 October 2008.

12 Rupert Hoare, 'A Meditation for Christmas 2008', unpublished, and used with Rupert's kind permission.

13 James MacMillan, 'The divine spark of music', Sandford St Martin Trust 30th Anniversary Lecture, 1 September 2008.

14 Andrew Motion interviewed by Andrew Rumsey, *Third Way*, vol. 32, no. 3, April 2009, p. 20.

15 Motion interviewed by Rumsey, p. 19.

16 Alain de Botton interviewed by Nick Spencer, *Third Way*, vol. 32, no. 4, May 2009, p. 18.

17 De Botton interviewed by Spencer, p. 18.

18 Gray, 'atheist delusion'.

8 November: the triumph of hope and Twitter

1 Barack Obama, Super Tuesday speech, Chicago, 5 February 2008.

2 Hanif Kureishi, *Something to Tell You*, London: Faber & Faber, 2008, p. 20.

3 Walter Brueggemann, 'The Power of dreams in the Bible', The *Christian Century*, 28 June 2005, pp. 28–31.

4 Brueggemann, 'Power of dreams in the Bible'.

5 Genesis 28.10–17.

6 Brueggemann, 'Power of dreams in the Bible'.

7 Genesis 41.1–36.

8 Brueggemann, 'Power of dreams in the Bible'.

9 Daniel 4.4–37.

10 Matthew 2.13–15.

11 Andrew Motion interviewed by Andrew Rumsey, *Third Way*, vol. 32, no. 3, April 2009, p. 19.

12 John Gray, 'The atheist delusion', *The Guardian*, 15 March 2008.

13 Dick Sheppard, quoted in Malcolm Johnson, *St Martin-in-the-Fields*, Chichester: Phillimore, 2005, p. 47.

14 Brueggemann, 'Power of dreams in the Bible'.

15 Barack Obama, *The Audacity of Hope: Thoughts on Reclaiming the American Dream*, New York: Crown, 2006, p. 207.

16 Obama, *Audacity of Hope*, p. 352.
17 Brueggemann, 'Power of dreams in the Bible'.

10 January: kissing you

1 'Kissing you', by Des'ree and Timothy Atak, from *William Shakespeare's Romeo + Juliet: Music from the Motion Picture*, Capitol, 1996. Lyrics by Des'ree Weekes © Sony/ATV Music Publishing. All rights reserved. Used by permission. Permission also sought from Westbury Music.
2 Matthew 27.46.
3 James Woodward, 'Love without pain is a lie', *Church Times*, 20 March 2008.
4 Joan Didion, *The Year of Magical Thinking*, New York: Knopf, 2005.
5 Susannah Clapp, *The Observer*, 14 May 2008.
6 Rosemary Lain-Priestley, 'Poem for dad', February 2006, unpublished.
7 Victoria Coren, *The Observer*, 31 August 2008.
8 *A Mighty Heart*, Paramount Vantage, 2007.
9 Menna Elfyn, 'Brooch (in memory of Stephanie Macleod)', in Menna Elfyn, *Perfect Blemish: New and Selected Poems 1995–2007*, Tarset: Bloodaxe Books, 2007; trans. Elin ap Hywel, 1996.
10 Woodward, 'Love without pain is a lie'.

11 February: adding laughter

1 Mark 10.14.
2 'Young people growing strong: the role of positive, structured activities', NCH Briefing, September 2007, p. 2.
3 Richard Layard and Judy Dunn, *A Good Childhood: Searching for Values in a Competitive Age*, London: Penguin, 2009.
4 Genesis 18.14.
5 Daniel Ladinsky (trans.), *The Gift: Poems by Hafiz the Great Sufi Master*, New York: Arkana, 1999. From the Penguin publication *The Gift: Poems by Hafiz*, copyright 1999 Daniel Ladinsky and used with his permission.

12 March again: the sublime in the ridiculous

1 Mahmoud Darwish, 'The dice player' (excerpt), trans. Fady Joudah, *The Guardian*, 16 August 2008. Reproduced by permission.
2 Exodus 3.1–6.
3 Mark 10.46–52.
4 John 4.1–42.
5 John 2.3–7.

6 Douglas Board, 'Seeing and not seeing', sermon for Homelessness Sunday, St Martin-in-the-Fields, 1 February 2009.

7 Anne Dyer, at the National Association of Diocesan Advisers in Women's Ministry Conference, 2008.

8 Andrew Motion interviewed by Andrew Rumsey, *Third Way*, vol. 32, no. 3, April 2009, p. 19.

9 The poem was quoted in full in the *Church Times*, 2 May 2008. I have omitted the first three lines, and am indebted to Andrew Motion for his personal permission to quote from the poem here.

10 Alain de Botton interviewed by Nick Spencer, *Third Way*, vol. 32, no. 4, May 2009, p. 18.

Conclusion

1 Fred Pratt Green, 'For the fruit of all creation', reproduced by permission of Stainer and Bell Ltd, London, England, <www.stainer.co.uk>.